SUMMIT YOUR EVEREST

YOUR COACH FOR OBSTACLE AND FAILURE MANAGEMENT

www.summityoureverest.com

ALSO BY KRISHNA SAGAR

AUDIO TRAINING TITLES

Empower your decision making

Emotional Intelligence

Due for release — Audio Titles

— Effective Communication

— Relationship Management

— Attitude Management

— Team Management

— Stress Management

SUMMIT YOUR EVEREST

YOUR COACH FOR OBSTACLE AND FAILURE MANAGEMENT

KRISHNA SAGAR (Ph.D), M.B.A, M.P.M, D.A.Pr, D.Psy

One of the leading Corporate Strategy and Success Coach in the world

MATRIX MEDIA

Hyderabad
www.matrixnova.com

Published by **Matrix Mentoring Pvt. Ltd.,**
103, Parkside, Road No.3, Banjara Hills,
Hyderabad-500 034
media@matrixnova.com
www.matrixnova.com

Published in arrangement with
Matrix Media
Hyderabad, India

SUMMIT YOUR EVEREST
ISBN 978-81-907512-0-9

First Matrix Media Impression:2008

Printed by
Tirumala Comprints Limited,
16-11-20/E, Saleem Nagar,
Malakpet, Hyderabad-36.
www.tirumalacomprints.com

I dedicate this book to my Mother & all those
men and women who strive to live their full potential everyday,
by courageously overcoming their obstacles & failure.
Thereby setting highest standards for others to follow.

CONTENTS

ACKNOWLEDGEMENTS

I am profoundly thankful to many who have made this book possible. This one page will not be sufficient to acknowledge my gratitude. However, I will attempt.

Mr. Rajiv Beri of Mac Millan India for his encouragement to initiate this book. Prof.Arun Tiwari to have helped me to interact personally and extract quotes from the former president of India Dr.A.P.J.Abdul Kalam. It was a remarkable meeting.

Meeting Barack Obama while he was campaigning for his primaries in New York was another highlight and his insights are inimitable and inspiring, I am forever thankful for those invaluable moments.

I am extremely touched by the gesture of General K.V. Krishna Rao, the former chief of Indian Army and former Governor of Jammu & Kashmir to have kindly consented and narrated the foreword as he was not well disposed at that time to write it.

I extend my gratitude to all those winners I have chosen from various fields. I thank them for their kindness to have spent time personally with me and allowing me to quote them. Their quotes are the life line for the reader in this book.

I am indebted to the help and encouragement extended by my dear friends and well wishers Dr.Kondal Rao, Surender Rao, Krishna Kishore, Prakash, Manish Malpani, Jagapathi Babu, Nadeemuddin, Venki Mahadevan, Agam Rao, Anuradha Venkatesh, Hamed Saberi, Kashif Suleman, Rahul Bajaj, Piyush Sahu, Seeta Murthy, Dr.Sudha, Vasudev Chaturvedi, Neelima, Ravi Vadlamani, Anju Poddar, Pinky Reddy, Naresh Raman, Kartic Godavarthy,

Jojan Thomas, Madhu Yashki Goud, Vice Admiral Balachandran, Gopala Krishna, Rajen Girgilani, Rajesh Pamnani, Dr.Venkat Ramana, General Mahajan, Charles-Colombo, Karin Trieber, Gale Naughton- SDSU, Caramen Bianchi-SDSU, Bob-USA, Supriya Kalia, Gangadhar Ramu, Pinninti Ashok, Jyothi, Dr.Mohan Rao and many others, who have supported and inspired me throughout.

My dear wife Pratibha, who was forever motivating and helping me with her critical but sharp editing support prior to professional editing rounds. My ever active entertainer 4 year old son Sahas Sagar to have put up with my long stints of absence for sabbaticals in Colombo and USA. Their support to me is invaluable.

Finally my publishers Matrix Media, the editorial team, personal and office team who have spent long hours with me for the last 2 years, Bhaskar, Satish, Sharif, Nidhi Negi, Aditya, Deepika, Sruthi, Harsha, Siddhika, Venu Gopal, Anil & Bhanu, Praveen Diddi, Shilpa, Raghuveer Rao, Indrani and several others.

I feel honored to have so many friends and colleagues whom I have recognized and many others who have contributed to the book in one way or the other and I extend my heart felt gratitude for their continued support.

***

FOREWORD
[As narrated to the Author]

I had my share of obstacles at every phase of my life, in my military career, as a governor and even in the personal domain. I believe no one is immune to obstacles. However, the way you manage them, actually determines your character.

Losing my mother while I was just a 14 days child at the beginning of my life & losing my wife at a very crucial phase of my life very recently, were some of the daunting obstacles in my life.

Army is built for obstacle management; soldiers are trained just to do that. 'My Country, Above Everything' is what we are taught all life. No obstacles should matter before the call of duty to defend the nation.

I have always taken obstacles head on and planned to overcome them with preparation and courage. I could always manage to stand up to my values and express 'what my obstacles are' and overcome them. Nothing stopped me from achieving goals which I had set for my nation and me.

My experience of fighting in the Second World War to all the Indian wars till date, has taught me some tough lessons on managing incredulous obstacles. My empathy and clarity of aim at all times helped me.

As the governor of Jammu & Kashmir, I had to set and achieve large and complex goals for the national security and integrity of this country. Some of the obstacles like the terrorism in Kashmir, while trying to conduct elections even attracted assassination attempts on my life, but I went on to overcome them to reach the assigned goals and took the state to elections.

None of the obstacles could stop me from preparing the state for elections and bringing this troubled state to partial normalcy during that time. There are innumerable instances of successful obstacle management in my eventful life. I have given my very best in life for all spheres and continue to do so even now.

I do believe very strongly that understanding obstacles & failures is crucial to building one's character and eventually to succeed.

Gen.K.V.Krishna Rao

Former Chief of Indian Army

Former Governor Nagaland, Manipur, Tripura, Jammu & Kashmir

***

PRELUDE

Everyone in this world would have experienced obstacles and some, even failure. Apparently, we all acknowledge that success is very intricately linked with obstacles & failure. We are very much aware of many legendary factoids of men and women, who after facing overwhelming obstacles and even dismal failure have attained historic success and resurrected themselves.

Yet, everyday millions of men and women across the world do feel depressed at even smallest obstacles. Many quit their long nurtured dreams, give up goals, destroy relationships, yield to situations, hurt others, hurt themselves, abandon positivity and some, even choose death as an extreme measure, in their attempt to avoid an obstacle or a failure.

Effective Obstacle & Failure management is the most sought after capability for any individual to succeed in the current times either in an organizational, family or a community setting.

I write this book with immense respect, admiration and fascination I personally have towards all those men and women, who despite all odds and adversity continue to set higher standards for themselves and others. They live with empowering values and beliefs, set grand goals, act with focus to accomplish results, which add value to themselves and others. I do believe with all humility that I belong to this fraternity. I write with my inherent analytical capability to break down complex processes into simple, understandable and applicable methods.

I remember my mother telling very early in my life, that 'You learn more from failures than from success' and I have figured very early that success most of the time is the outcome of the past learning from failure.

I grew up to find it's so true. Especially after spending more than a decade of traveling the world to coach men and women ranging from Armed forces to Politics, from Doctors to Scientists, from Corporate Leaders to Business Patriarchs, from Business Students to Entrepreneurs, from communities to service organizations in the areas relevant to their strategic growth, as a part of my profession as a corporate coach & strategy consultant.

This journey is interspersed with so much of learning from shared experiences of all these groups and mostly their experiences of facing obstacles, claims of failure, and the pride of overcoming tough obstacles, and tales of resurrection from failures. This journey continues...

In the times we live in, effective role models in this area of focus are not just scarce but even endangered. My attempt through this book is to highlight the key factors essential for effective management and to project many men and women amongst us, who have with their conscious efforts to overcome obstacles and failures have, in the process set higher standards to themselves and others to live by.

In my personal interaction with many of these tough and intelligent people, I have extracted quotes from their insights, which I am enlisting in this book; they can guide and inspire you for lifelong application. Many of these winners could well be made role models for effective management of obstacles & failure.

This book is my focused attempt to deal with a subject which is, as important as life. The knowledge and application of which, can make a lifelong difference.

I believe very strongly, from the first stage of our life till the last, all that we do mostly is managing obstacles & failure, to make way for progress of any kind in our lives.

I am writing this book to make it a personal coach for you, your family, and your teams and for the community you live in. I am left no stone unturned in this attempt to give you high quality and tested inputs. Meeting and interacting with several winners personally to get their quotes especially for this book, gathering experiential references & research outcomes, and to provide you universally relevant, applicable solutions for Obstacle & Failure management.

As you read this book from first chapter to the last, you will experience the depth I traveled to bring out the most effective solutions for Obstacle & Failure management for you.

This book is the result of two decades of my experiential learning and about four years of focused research in this area. I urge you to read this entire book and see if there is any obstacle & failure, you cannot manage, ever.

***

THE TITLE – 'SUMMIT YOUR EVEREST'

Standing as the world's tallest peak over 29000 ft above the sea level, Mount Everest is a magnificent symbol of the tallest physical obstacle, which challenges the indomitable human will.

I consider 'Mount Everest' symbolizes all those obstacles in our life which are large, which belittle, challenge and even overwhelm us. The 'Summit' is also symbolic to how few amongst us can successfully overcome this great obstacle with their conviction & action.

The 29th of May 1953 marks a historic day for humanity, when the mountaineers Edmond Hillary & Tenzing Norgay conquered the peak for the first time ever. It's a testament to two facts. The first is, no one till then focused on that goal as hard and backed it with the spirit and action as the successful duo and the second fact, a huge visual & mental limitation was broken in the mind sets of hundreds of men & women that day.

In the scripted history, when no man or woman ever summited this peak for till 1953, in just few years after that summit by Sir Edmond Hillary & Norgay, there were hundreds who have overcome this huge obstacle. Now you tell me, what changed? The obstacle or the mindset?....You are absolutely right.

For me, Everest is not just the world's tallest peak but a visual metaphor of a huge set of obstacles, which could even lead to failures. I strongly believe & the same will be in focus through out this book, that if we do not recognize the limitations & obstacles inside us and surmount them, it would be quite a task to overcome many obstacles which exist outside.

I am certain that the successful first climbers achieved this feat first in their mind before they actually did it in real. And all those winners after these two great men today are doing just the same, they know they can do it, as someone else have already proven the possibility.

The book name proposes that you overcome your own Everest internally before even attempting to overcome the one outside. Win over your internal obstacles.

'If you find a path with no obstacles, it probably doesn't lead anywhere.'

***

THE NEED – WHY THIS BOOK ?

There are hundreds of books on Success management available on the book shelves and hardly any on obstacle & failure management work published till date. I am of the view 'Obstacle & Failure Management' precedes 'Success Management' and thought of giving the 'Devil its due'. On a more serious note, I personally feel and you will agree, that if we look around, we find many grappling with lack of understanding of obstacles, losing all hope on failures , and mismanaging several personal and professional resources without a scientific approach to goal setting process.

I feel most our current problems have to do with the way we understand & define our obstacles, assess the implications of management & mismanagement and an action plan to overcome the same. There is an impending need to understand this invaluable concept with objectivity and focus to manage effectively.

Success and failure are inseparable constituents. Everyone talks of subjectivity in defining these two vital components of life. While agreeing on the subjectivity aspect, I, wish to differ in the impossibility to find innumerable commonalities despite subjectivity to define Success, Failure & Obstacles objectively. Through this book I have attempted to do just that.

I feel the only way to increase the possibility of success in one's life is to gain clarity on 'Goals' and the process of setting them, redefining obstacles & failures and by effectively managing these factors to keep accomplishing Success.

As you move into the next growth phase of your life, at every stage you are presented with new obstacles. This book can help you demystify those obstacles and help you understand that most of the obstacles are driven by our internal fundamentals & drivers, and these two critical factors need to be strengthened to effectively overcome one's obstacles & failures.

From an obstacle such as rush hour traffic to an obstacle like spouse's irrational behavior you failed to change over years, to a financial obstacle which is threatening your dreams of building a secured life, to a personal obstacle of lack of drive to solve problems at the first exposure, to an obstacle of time for project deadlines or any other obstacle you could think of, your life presents an array of obstacles everyday for you to manage.

Many struggle without focus in either understanding an obstacle or redefining it to suit their needs. Many do morph, deceive themselves and others by concealing, some take a detour, some avoid, some escape, some postpone, some even apply ineffective, irrational & emotional measures to overcome and some quit.

There are very few, who can effectively encounter, experience and overcome obstacles and failures consistently to attain 'Success'. No wonder, there are only a handful in the world that are extremely successful.

It's an everyday attempt to overcome these internal & external obstacles, which lead you to reach your goals. This book helps you do precisely that. By now, I hope you are convinced of the need to have a book in this focus area.

***

"Obstacle & Failure management is crucial for any form of Success in Life."

- Dr. A.P.J.Abdul Kalam, Former President of India

FUNDAMENTALS

FUNDAMENTALS

While life is an exciting opportunity, the twists and turns you can experience can be highly adventurous or highly painful depending on how you shape your path towards your goals. I believe most of what you make out of your life, depends on 'you'.

Success, Obstacles and Failures are a part of moving ahead in life, they are inseparable factors and have to be managed, if one needs to maintain a peaceful, progressive and a happy life.

I don't believe in quick fix solutions and I hope you respect it too. I wish to lead you into deeper understanding, through breaking it down into easily understandable components.

Let's move straight into the subject. The model presented below represents variety of factors which drive action and produce results. The interpretation of results as Success, Failure or Obstacles, presents us an opportunity to manage that eventually.

Please go over this model and as the chapter explains all the components in this pictorial expression, it gives you more clarity.

After completing this chapter, I urge you to revisit the model and analyze further to gain deeper understanding of the proposed process. You could very well try relating this model to your own journey towards your goals. That will greatly help understand your current stage and the subsequent impact of obstacles & failures on you.

SOF Model [Success, Obstacle & Failure]

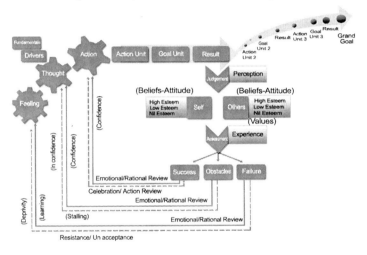

This model clearly explains how the fundamentals & drivers [Which I will explain later] impact through FTA [Feelings, Thoughts & Actions], in the flow of action towards goals.

Success, obstacles and failures in this model are purely subjective analysis of results. They seem to differ from one individual to other and so does the outcome.

This model will clarify the flow, the analysis and the 'results' driven by 'fundamentals' and 'drivers'.

The flow of the Model

You will understand this better after reading the 'Fundamentals' & 'Drivers' in this chapter.

Stage-1

❖   The FTA [feelings, thoughts and actions] drive the primary flow with 'Fundamentals & Drivers' supporting the initial action.

❖   'Drivers' have a unique impact on every stage of this Model.

Stage-2

❖   All action is driven through action units towards smaller goals called 'Goal units' to reach a Grand Goal.

❖   Every action unit on a goal unit drives a 'Result', through a 'Perception' driven judgement.

❖   Fundamentals such as 'Attitude', plays a crucial role in the process of 'Judgement'.

❖   Fundamentals such as beliefs and values impact 'self' and 'others' judgement which result as 'experience' driven 'assessment'.

❖   Success, obstacles or failures is the outcome of the flow driven by the fundamental 'emotions'.

Stage-3

❖   If one's experience assessment is 'success' the possibility is a quick acceptance with a feeling of 'celebration' and analysis of 'action review' which eventually results in 'confidence'. Success can at times also effect in delay of future action towards the next goal unit, with either prolonged 'celebration' mode or with overconfidence, which can lead to delays & obstacles.

"Success to me is about attaining a certain sensibility that one finds within oneself. This sensibility is something I cannot measure or define. It is about a particular moment, an instance, an expression, an experience that is realized."

- Kishore Biyani, Chairman, Future Group

❖   If one's experience assessment is 'obstacle', there are two possibilities, one being an emotional and rational review resulting in training, realignment, regrouping or redirection resulting in further action. The other possibility can be emotional incapacitation leading to long delays in future actions with inconfidence and indecisiveness.

❖   If one's experience assessment is 'failure', there are again two possibilities, an emotional and rational review resulting in acceptance with less resistance and the second possibility can be an emotional incapacitation leading to further deterioration of emotions resulting in either stalling or extremely delayed actions through extreme inconfidence and indecisiveness.

No wonder the phrase 'Success breeds Success', looks so justified with this model, as the emotions of success, can most often than not, if well directed can result in more success, acting as a catalyst. While the failure, unless challenged and managed effectively can easily drive an individual into further failures through inconfidence and indecisiveness.

It's very important to understand the fundamentals & drivers to understand obstacles & manage them, let's dig deeper into understanding the impact.

Fundamentals

If you wish to effectively overcome obstacles & failures to succeed in reaching your goals, you might have to patiently walk with me through the entire book. I don't believe there are any quick fix solutions and short cuts, if you plan to acquire scientific and lasting solutions.

The best way to move forward is from the bottom to top. In this chapter, I will take you through the 'Four Fundamentals', these factors can be the reason why we encounter obstacles and surprisingly modifying the same and reapplying them against obstacles can help you overcome them. Let's call it 'Reverse Impact'.

It's challenging at one end and intriguing at the other, to focus on these 'Fundamentals' as they come across, as isolated concepts but as you focus and connect through this chapter, you will find an amazing and intricate relationship between each.

All four of these Fundamentals are core ingredients of your personality and thereby has strong conditioning effect personally and socially. Infact, each of these and together actually personify your identity in personal and social settings.

Imagine how important are these questions - How are your emotions impacting you? What are your beliefs? What are your core values? And what's your state of mind ? At any given point of time, these questions have a lot to say about who you actually are.

"Obstacles are likely to slow the decision making. In the case of a failure the individual may question his or her ability to make good decisions in the future hence he or she becomes "stuck" in an indecisive mode. In the case of obstacles, if the individual feels overwhelmed then I believe a common reaction is to do nothing."

- Prof. Kathleen A Krentler, Professor,
San Diego State University, USA

There is a need to understand the finer details of the Obstacles prior to managing them. In the first few chapters, we will attempt to demystify the core factors that cause obstacles and in the later ones, we can understand how to use these factors to manage obstacles & failures effectively.

FUNDAMENTALS

❖ Emotions

❖ Beliefs

❖ Values

❖ Attitude

EMOTIONS

"Emotions can play havoc with you, in the times of adversity. They can unsettle your composure and capabilities"

- Vijaya Rama Rao, Former CBI Director & Minister of State

It happened in 1982, in the Asian Games Hockey Championship, when India and Pakistan were fighting for the cup in a nail biting crucial finale, India lost to Pakistan. The passionate hockey fans, media and the sports fraternity, unable to digest that colossal loss had instantly and passionately with impunity branded the captain of the Indian Hockey Team Mr. Meer Ranjan Negi as the traitor who sold the match to Pakistan. This allegation is founded on baseless imagination of match fixing for his personal, financial gains.

The emotions after that allegation and their impact and backlash was so huge, not only that he had to abandon the sport he loved the most, but also his home and his neighborhood, so was the size and degree of the obstacle in the form of an emotion.

"After the Asian games debacle, I was so deeply disturbed as I was very young. I even thought of committing suicide.

- Mir Ranjan Negi, Former Captain, Indian National Hockey

As you can understand, the largest obstacle to Mr.Negi at that time was 'a set of emotions' - Anger, unleashed by the sports fans, the result of this obstacle was also 'a set of emotions' which Negi felt - depressed, abused, distrusted, disrespected, deprived that could have lead him to a disastrous failure, if not for his tenacious attempts to overcome this adversity to resurrect himself.

Today, he is a house hold name in India with a box office hit like 'Chak de India' made in inspiration of his life played by the super star of Indian cinema Sharukh Khan and his continued presence on several TV shows. What a change ... time and timely management of Obstacles & Failures can make to one's life !

Emotions are what we immediately experience, when encounter obstacles of any type, degree and size. They are the ones which help and also the ones that hurt the process of managing obstacles. The impact of emotions on the obstacle management is so crucial, if you knock off this one chapter out of this book, it would not justify writing the rest. I hope you got the emphasis on this Fundamental.

So, let's understand 'Emotions' to gain clarity in order to assess implications and draw strategies from this fundamental at the next level.

Let me focus on explaining 'Emotions' as it is generally used as 'Feelings'.

"Emotions are what makes or breaks the strength of will to succeed. I do feel, emotions are crucial to be managed in times of severe obstacles & failures."

- Madhu Yaskhi Goud, Member of Parliament

The basis of all human activity is emotions. All action in your life...I mean every action, is in response to an emotion or to satisfy one.

While I make this profound statement, I want you to relate to very basic physiological actions like breathing, quenching thirst, satisfying hunger, sleeping, making love, to... some middle order actions like Socializing, Partying, Shopping, Competing, Complaining, Blaming to extreme emotions like Anger, Frustration, Depravity, Vengeance, Desperation, Jealousy are all emotions of different degrees. Some are very basic and some are medium and some are extreme.

e your imagination on the above and the se actions, you can also figure out the resultant ns are performed.

ɟ with one such analysis...I know you will be able to do the rest.

I feel suffocated if I don't breathe, I feel 'choked' if I don't breathe, I feel 'breathless'... and when I breathe - I feel 'relieved'. I feel 'alive'. I feel 'rejuvenated'. The highlighted ones are emotions. I know it's not that hard to understand emotions with all the help you have got.

Think about this, when we talk of large obstacles, we are assigning a degree to it, isn't it ? Large. How did we arrive at that degree is basically by assessing the impact of that obstacle on our emotions & subsequent consequences ? Emotions are very crucial in Obstacle assessment.

Let's go ahead and define Emotion, for structured understanding 'An emotion / feeling is the internal or external response to internal or external stimulus, which is spontaneous, natural, and consistent.'

The 'stimulus/response' might sound complex at the first instance but pretty simple to understand. If the temperature in a room is hot, there is an external stimulus 'temperature', which triggers an emotion internally 'Warm / hot Feeling', when expressed externally, it can be 'I feel hot in this room', as simple.

As referred in the definition, the 'spontaneity' in the definition is about the natural impulse and independence of an emotion as it does not depend on any factor to be 'felt'. Feelings just happen. For example: Feeling of Love is similar in India and so it is in USA. Feeling of Hunger by someone in Somalia is as some would feel in London. The basic feelings remain almost same across the world, despite the outcomes might differ, as they are spontaneous and are natural impulses and are independent.

"The corner stone of all Failure management is Emotional Management."

- Prof. Rammohan Rao, Dean, Indian School of Business [ISB]

The dimension 'Natural & Consistent' in the definition points to the characteristic of emotions, as they are so real & natural that unless they are faked consciously, they cannot be debated or questioned. For example: A head of the state has made a statement recently - "Iraqi's shouldn't feel 'Occupied', they should feel 'Liberated'."

You cannot dictate other people's feelings. It demonstrates the utter lack of understanding of Emotions and their implications.

Emotional Sequencing

Emotion - Options - Emotion - Options

Please go through this sequencing, most of the time, the kind of options you raise are crucial to assess your capability to manage or mismanage obstacles. Let me explain.

The way one responds to any obstacle primarily is through emotions. They are the first outcomes. What type of emotions and what degree of emotions would one experience depends on the type and degree of the obstacle, which we will discuss in the later chapters.

There's a certain amount of conditioned response to Obstacles or failures which accompany us either through our childhood upbringing, by our role models or through our understanding of the obstacles & failures or the lack of it.

At this stage it's important to understand that 'Emotions' could be double edged as Fundamentals.

At one end, if you are prone to extreme emotional response on encountering even small obstacles, you can imagine the response to large obstacles, and I leave it to your imagination, the reaction to failures.

No wonder there are many individuals who exaggerate small issues and feel tense about it all day and also make others around unstable. This propensity to react with exaggerated emotions can lead you to encounter 'huge obstacles' on the path towards your goals.

On the other hand, you can apply this fundamental by design to overcome any type or degree of obstacles & failures. I want you to go back into past to recall having overcome any major obstacle in your life.

You will certainly be able to figure out, your feelings of resoluteness, confidence, decisiveness and positivity would have helped you accomplish this task. It's almost impossible to overcome obstacles and failures without managing emotions and being able to use effective emotions in the course of testing times.

If you experience higher degree emotions at even smaller degree obstacles, you are bound to perceive the obstacle as larger in size and feel more disempowering emotions, which are of further higher degree and which could be devastating and not helpful in managing obstacles.

If you focus back on Mr.Ranjan Negi's life, the way he has managed very high degree obstacles over a long period of time to make a successful comeback. You will find a pattern this role model has adopted and that is the model I am proposing for utilizing this fundamental 'emotions' for managing obstacles.

Building Options - Cycle of Emotions

'I do feel first before I think & act. When I express controversial facts either in parliament or in media sometimes against the regular norms. I believe as a young politician the need is to represent the feelings of my constituents at the Parliament. That's why I am elected.'

- Madhu Yashki Goud, Member of Parliament

The emotional cycle starts with experiencing a certain degree [low /high] emotions on encountering obstacles and which leads to loss of options or creation of more options before you to manage a situation you are facing.

Lack of options after an obstacle or failure can lead to 'down time' or unproductive time. This is the result of disempowering emotions, leading to slowdown in accomplishing goals and eventually failure, if continued as a regular emotional response.

Creation of options through empowering emotions can lead to correction, re-grouping and re-navigating the action on goals, in the advent of obstacles & failures. The possibility of success increases with this emotional response.

I will highlight the emotional strategies to overcome obstacles & failures, when we start finding solutions using these Fundamentals in the later chapters.

By now, I am certain that you are aware of the emotions and their impact on you as a fundamental.

This fundamental determines, if your emotions are empowering or disempowering, when you encounter and experience an obstacle or a failure. To overcome, you certainly need this fundamental to be an empowering one.

So the very first fundamental which drives any action in life towards a goal is an Emotion [Feeling]. If you focus on the SOF Model, it is the first fundamental, which drives 'Thoughts' & 'Actions'.

BELIEFS

"I believe, so I am "

- Barack Obama, President, USA

It's quite intriguing, if you probe into this fundamental which not only affects ones capability of managing obstacles but the entire frame work of life, we live on a daily basis.

Your beliefs define your core existence. 'I am an ambitious man', 'I am very knowledgeable', 'I am a hindu', ' I am patriotic', ' I am a responsible mother', 'I am a loving husband', 'I am a great boss', 'I am a responsible citizen', ' I am a great leader', 'I am not good looking', 'I am a looser', are all beliefs.

Each of this belief is based on references from ourselves and others. The stronger the quantum of reference, the stronger the belief. Weaker the reference, weaker the belief.

The strongest beliefs in you are those, which are strongly referenced and supported internally either through your experiences or through your regular and consistent action based on those beliefs. 'I am always right' is such a belief, which can create many obstacles, especially if it's a very strong internalized belief.

Interesting, isn't it? Let's probe further.

It will be surprising and shocking to know that almost all your thoughts are drawn out of your beliefs and all action is driven by the same.

Almost all our action in life is driven by our beliefs. So, don't you think, we need to be a little guarded and know how this fundamental will affect your actions towards obstacle & failure management.

Changing your beliefs is like taking a rebirth. By changing beliefs, you can possibly change any aspect of your life today. I mean it. Look at it this way, if you wish to change any one habit in your life, start by changing your past beliefs which are supporting that habit.

For example 'Smoking relieves my stress' is a belief, for me it's a disempowering belief as it is not founded on a scientific basis, to prove it true. But if you possess the above belief, you are bound to be a big smoker, and especially so if you are in a stressful job or a situation.

If you have to quit smoking, changing your belief to 'Smoking is very dangerous to my body & mind' or a belief like 'Smoking gets me less dates' or 'smoking ruins my respect with my children' helps. That's what eventually; those who quit anyways do after years of rehabilitation or counseling.

It's possible, even in an instant. By changing a belief, you can change almost anything and everything about you.

You could almost alter the path of your life and the grand goals, by just altering your beliefs in an instant.

It will be well within the context to site the examples of Gautama Buddha, Mahaveer, Valmiki, King Ashoka, and in the modern day context Mahatma Gandhi, Martin Luther King Jr, Nelson Mandela, Mother Teresa or even Barack Obama to prove how instantly by shifting beliefs someone's life can change towards different direction impacting their life and others.

"My attitude and confidence cannot be shaken by any situation."

- Mrs. Seetha Murthy, Principal, Silver Oaks School

In reference to obstacle & failure management, I certainly feel understanding the impact of beliefs will give you immense leverage to apply this fundamental in any situation which might challenge you, as an obstacle or a failure.

Infact it helps immensely first to understand what are your current beliefs of what constitute 'Obstacles' & 'Failure', this understanding can be the starting and ending point of gaining all the needed capabilities to manage obstacles & failures.

If your beliefs can be designed by you, instead of going by the beliefs which you possess by default, you can use them to suit the needs at any time to reach goals despite any adversity. You can possibly overcome most of the obstacles & failure effectively and succeed.

Belief Composition

"I trust if someone says he can, he will."

–Prof. Adrian Kennedy,
Managing Director, Wellness RX Apollo

Most of our beliefs can be classified as 'External' and 'Internal Beliefs' based on where our beliefs are supported from.

No one is born with beliefs. You acquire them as you grow, through your childhood upbringing, schooling, parenting and the macro environment which you live in and situations you face through your formative period of growth.

So, it's pretty clear that all beliefs are 'external' to start with, but as we act on them, we 'internalize' them. The strongest beliefs are those, which are consistently acted upon. That means all those internalized beliefs are the strongest, in your system. They are also the hardest to change.

If you have certain beliefs, which are not internalized, for example- you do believe 'Truth is a great virtue' but do not practice it in your everyday life, which means you lie often. The above belief then is just an external belief, as it has come from outside and still not internalized by you. So it is not strong and easy to change.

I want you to picture this. A wooden chair with four legs & each leg representing an experience of acting on a 'belief'. If the seating plank is the Reference Platform, the set of all your past experiences of a certain belief, your belief is sitting right on the top of it.

Let's imagine hypothetically that 'Non-Voilence' is a belief of Mahatma Gandhi, and is sitting on this chair.

17

The legs of the chair then can be labeled as 'E' on each, which stands for External Reference. As you are already aware, all beliefs are External to start with.

The first time Gandhi applied this belief and acted on it, one of the legs would turn 'I' [Internal] marking the process of internalizing a belief. The result of that action will impact his belief, to act or not to act with this belief again in future. If Mahatma Gandhi were to stop acting on that belief called 'Non-Voilence' interpreting the resultant violence on him by British as an ineffective or a negative outcome of his belief called 'Non Voilence', that would have been external & not strong.

But infact, Gandhi's continuous usage of that belief till the end of his life is a testament to the fact that he interpreted the outcomes of his beliefs to be successful and continuously & consistently acted on that belief. If there could be one belief which can personify Gandhi, it's his belief of 'Non-Violence'.

So, if you wish to analyze his 'belief composition', it would be a highly internalized belief with a minimum of 3 I's on the reference legs. A very strong and empowering belief.

No wonder, any amount of external aggression, delayed results, imprisonment and seclusion could impact his belief till the end, he has overcome innumerable hurdles and obstacles with this strong belief.

I suppose it's not very hard now to comprehend that, strongly internalized beliefs are not impacted by external influences and non internalized beliefs are impacted by external influences.

So, while we are glad that internal beliefs are strong and can resist external impact and are relatively hard to change, I hope you would want them to be 'Empowering Beliefs'.

I strongly recommend, you do a Belief Audit for assessing the current 'Belief Composition' on your primary beliefs and see if your empowering beliefs are internalized or your disempowering beliefs are internalized.

You could do this to your family members , team or colleagues to understand the 'Why' of behavior and recommend changes.

Though I am very eager to share more analytical inputs on Beliefs , the focus for sure is on the application of what we have already gathered on 'Obstacle & Failure Management'. So, let's move on the next fundamental.

Belief Audit Sheet

My Empowering Beliefs:

1. _____

2. _____

3. _____

4. _____

5. _____

6. _____

My Disempowering Beliefs

1. _____

2. _____

3. _____

4. _____

5. _____

6. _____

My Strongly Internalized Beliefs [From the above list]

My Externalized Beliefs [From the above list]

VALUES

Please take a piece of paper and start writing what's the top priority of your life at this phase. What is important to you in the order of your priority?

To help you, I am quoting few priorities. You can choose yours or add new.

❖ Work

❖ Money

❖ Family

❖ Health

❖ Respect

❖ Holiday

❖ Power

❖ Fame

❖ Freedom

❖ Truth

❖ Peace

❖ Relationships

What are values?

If you have chosen the order of priority from the above, the list represents your values. Values are defined by different people differently; some refer values to morals & ethics, some as cultural ethos and some as sacrosanct ideals.

In my understanding, values are 'what are valuable to you'. I believe these priorities also keep shifting over the period of our time, they get refined and mature and also get rearranged at different phases of one's life.

"It's values, which are tested the most, while you encounter obstacles or failures."

- Pinniti Ashok, Government Pleader, Attorney at Law

What are my top 5 values at the age of 18 might not remain so at the age of 35 and what is at 35 might not be at 80. I hope I drove home the point. At every phase of life, there are certain values which outdo others in their importance. And there is nothing wrong with it and it's very natural.

To make this definition easier to understand, I want you to focus on your current goals. List the top 5 goals you have now, and if I am not wrong, all your current prioritized goals are driven by your prioritized values.

For example, if one of my current goals is 'To shed 3 kgs of body weight in this month to look slimmer', one of your top values will be 'health'.

If another goal is 'to buy a BMW X6 by the end of the year', one of your top value will be 'Money' or 'Identity', 'Luxury' or even all the three in an order.

What you value most are 'values'. The priorities which you would want to support 'no matter what' in that phase of your life. When you can support these priorities, you feel better and happy. When you cannot support them you feel restless or stressed.

If you pay close attention to the phase of your life, where you were very happy, it would be when you were able to support your core values to the best. In contrary, all sadness, unhappiness and stress in life can be attributed to your inability to support your values at that period of time.

Values either constrict or liberate you. However, nobody can dictate what must be your values, it's you who need to work on whether your values at any period of time empowered you or disempowered you to utilize resources to the best of your capabilities.

If I look at my own 'value sequence', it's not the same a year ago. There has been a small shuffle of priorities, but most of my primary values remain constant. Across life priorities change, as one value precedes other as per the need, but as long as you can support those priorities in order, you could very well be on the path to success. In fact that is the feeling outcome of success.' Your capability to support your values'.

You could take example of Mahatma Gandhi, Martin Luther King Jr, or contemporary legends like Arnold Schwarzenegger or Barack Obama to assess their values across their life, despite slight change of priorities.

Both Gandhi and King had 'Freedom' and 'Respect' as the primary values for almost all their life. Arnold seem to have 'Recognition', 'Work' and 'Wealth', while Obama seems to have 'compassion' and 'adding value to others'. Each of their goals is directly representing their order of values, if you have paid attention.

Values are transferable

Yeah, you can change your values; Infact they do usually get transformed for many across various life phases. At times obstacles & failures can force you, compel you or even motivate you to make changes in your value sequence or sometimes even add or delete values.

Someone who has been running behind money keeping it as a first value can shift to a lower stage after experiencing a heart stroke. 'Health' can become his primary value instantly after that incident.

An event on the train in South Africa has shifted Mahatma Gandhi's value priority, from 'work' to 'freedom' and 'respect'.

The 'Value List' and 'Value Sequence' are important factors to look out for one's value assessment. In future chapters, when we start applying this fundamental to overcome obstacles & failure, changes to value list and value sequence will be proposed to strengthen you in the times of adversity.

You can look at some examples of some infamous transformation of values too, especially in the western celebrity circuit. Legendary sports and music icons in the recent period of time are in the news for all the wrong reasons, either a drug abuse, relationship turmoil, bankruptcy, or an ugly scam. The reason for 'fall from grace' is simple. You know it by now. The value list and value sequencing issues lead them there.

I guess you have fathomed the power of Values. This is the fundamental which drives all goals, both micro and grand, one sets out to accomplish.

Empowering Values

"If one knows their values, they would never lose themselves."

– Dr. Kondal Rao, Chairman, Sister Nivedita Foundation

A set of values which drive you towards effectively utilizing your resources both internally and externally. They guide all your action towards your micro and grand goals.

The relationship with beliefs is so impactful for the value system. If I have a set of beliefs which help me support my values, I can attain empowerment easily.

Disempowering Values

These are a set of values, which drive you away from your micro and grand goals. These compel you to ineffectively utilize your internal and external resources.

If my beliefs don't support my values, the empowerment is lost and that's where the conflict begins.

"One of the best actions I love is to make money. For me it's a top value, but 'giving' is a greater value. So, I make as much money to give as much."

– Murali Mohan, Actor & Chairman, Jayabheri Group

As the value system and sequencing is a very personal process and is influenced by the kind of role models you have in your life, hardly anyone else can be blamed than you, for not having an 'empowered value system'.

"Knowing what is important for me and what is valuable has always helped me to get what I want."

- Manish Kumar Malpani, Director, Maheshwari Group

Value Sequencing Sheet

[Please put all your values from your list in an order of priority, as of now]

1. _____

2. _____

3. _____

4. _____

5. _____

6. _____

7. _____

8. _____

9. _____

10. _____

ATTITUDE

"One needs to have great amount of positive attitude and must think that he can overcome the obstacles. Of course the goals you set, needs to be sensible and achievable than being outlandish."

- Prof.Ram Mohan Rao, Dean, Indian School of Business [ISB]

Your attitude points to your beliefs and perception.

Sometimes you look at men and women who are physically or mentally challenged yet their 'attitude' is more effective to solve problems in comparison to their much endowed sane cousins. Their 'beliefs' have lead their 'perceptions' to be not intimidated by their shortcomings. That's how they function more efficiently. They focus on their strengths. Their attitude is resourceful and effective.

Attitude is a 'State of Mind'

Attitude is a state of mind. Effective attitude is an effective and resourceful state of mind, which has greater capability to utilize the internal & external resources of an individual.

Unresourceful attitude disadvantages you from effectively utilizing your internal and external resources. It also creates impediments to 'accountable action'.

One of the key attributes of a large obstacle or a failure is that it sets in the 'Unresourceful Attitude' at least for a while, and the capability of an effective Obstacle & Failure manager lies in staying the least time in this state of mind.

On one end, you see the young armed forces men & women, who live in challenging conditions in most of their assignments with

27

bare minimum necessities and still fight with patriotism and fervor for the nation without complaining. And on the other, you see some young city brats who hop pubs, drive plush cars, spend like there's no tomorrow, live in all comforts of material life but still complain.

The difference in these youngsters is their 'attitude towards life'.

The team leader who takes responsibility to all delays and failures of project deadlines and passes on all the credit to his fellows in the team has a resourceful attitude , in comparison to the one who hogs all the limelight and passes the buck to the team members, when chips are down.

A teacher, who allows the enquiry spirit in children, by allowing them to question her class room sessions, has the 'attitude to respect' a child as an individual, has a 'resourceful attitude' in comparison to a teacher who treats children like submissive recipients of knowledge from her.

Attitude is what makes the difference when similar situations are handled differently by two individuals leading to different results, one very effective and the other ineffective.

The Attitude Sequence

"The farther you escape, the harder they follow. You can't be an escapist."

- Salman Khan, Movie Actor

When you encounter any situation, your values and beliefs drive you to perceive that situation in a way someone else with a different set of beliefs and values might not. The subsequent reaction and results also reflect the difference in the way you both will manage that situation.

'In fact most of the obstacles & failures are the outcomes of ineffective handling of situations through our perception and attitude'.

'Resourceful Attitude' & 'Unresourceful Attitude' are the terms I will be using in the future chapters to drive strategies for effective management of obstacles and failures.

Building Options

"Life is very simple; it's we who make it complex."

- Jagapathi Babu, Movie Actor

Attitude works wonders with building options. It's the attitude which impacts the options we have before us. Imagine if you were in a resourceful attitude, the very presence in this state will present you with more options in comparison to someone who is operating from an unresourceful state.

In the chapters ahead, you will figure out the impact of more options on effective management of Obstacles and Failures.

If you are failing to choose, your are choosing to fail.

Reverse Impact Model - Fundamentals

This model exhibits the reverse impact of how the fundamentals can be impacted through FTA [Feelings/ Thoughts / Actions] to judge results as obstacles, failures and success and also how the resultant outcomes can equally impact the same factors, showcasing the reverse impact.

For example, a young executive with a set of actions towards his goal, if encounters an obstacle, it is imperative that the impact of the obstacle would also be on his feelings, thoughts and actions along with the beliefs, values and attitude.

"All those factors which create obstacles, can also be tools to manage them eventually, if applied differently"

- Venkimahadevan, Director, Motorola India

DRIVERS

2

D R I V E R S

Reverse Impact Model - Drivers

Congratulations, you have successfully crossed over from fundamentals. The next understanding we need to gain, is about what moves us ahead towards and what drags us away from our goals.

Just as how the 'fundamentals' have the dual role in both creating obstacles while they are ineffective and helping you overcome adversity, while they are effective, Drivers do share those characteristics.

Drivers can drive problems or solutions to you, depending upon their empowering and disempowering nature. As you go over these factors which influence your capabilities to overcome adversity and win wars, you will realize the role they play in shaping your destiny, in the true sense of the term 'drivers'.

If fundamentals are about 'who you are', drivers are about 'what you would eventually become'.

I don't need to request your keen attention to this chapter, do I?

DRIVERS

❖ Macro Perspective

❖ SMART Goals

❖ Focus

❖ Courage

❖ Accountable Action

Macro Perspective

Life will never be the same after the death of a loved one in any family. It can either bring to surface only the emotions of separation or it can also affect a paradigm shift by new understanding of life, leading to a macro perspective on life.

I vividly remember the first funeral I attended. I did not gain any new perspective of life with it; I was just 6 yrs old. The funeral I attended when I was 10 has triggered a shift of how I used to look at life, and another visit when I was 22 completed the cycle. The shift from a proud, everlasting, immortal, indestructible temperament about life to an aware, temporary, sensible, time bound, mortal and true understanding of what it means to live.

33

This transformation of 'thought' is neither guaranteed on your next 'Funeral Visit' nor can it be an everlasting enlightenment. The revelation can last a week and then you fall into the trap of your everyday routine and be back to square one, before you realize.

Infact it need not be just a funeral visit , which can trigger this shift in your thought process, it can happen anytime , at any age , any day , anywhere - 'only if you wish to gain a new perspective of life somewhere remotely in your mind'. It's essential and somehow, each one of us does get this realization at some point of time in life. The earlier, the better.

I recall what Mahatma Gandhi quoted once, "Life is, how you live it", there is immense depth to his contention that the entire experience is rather in your hands than, what is usually considered as destiny or in someone else's control.

Gaining a new perspective on Life

"I have not asked for life. I have no clue, how I have been granted this life. I have it now. So, why complain."

- Jagapathi Babu, Movie Actor

Cellular science, molecular biology, physiology, physics, chemistry & psychology have drawn scientific inferences that we evolved over billions of years from a single celled species to the current stage through various phases of evolution. 'The evolutionary model' by Darwin, suggests that we are the outcome of a long drawn game of the 'Survival of the fittest'.

The scientific inference that a human body is a multi-cellular, procreating, flexible, and continuously ageing and biologically time bound phenomenon is hard to digest for many.

Life has so many other attractive nuances and colorful emotional connotations than a plain bland scientific explanation. True, but it does not hurt to know, what we are in real, apart from all the roles we play in our everyday life, externally.

From a single cell zygote, to an embryo in foetus and to a fully formed human being with billions of functional and highly specialized cells, life of human is miraculous with its innumerable capabilities, complex organ structure, self sustenance and rate of growth.

I am rather in awe of the entire process of life, as much as I am in awe of the astronomical science. You would feel the same, if you pay little attention to who actually you are, how you got to this shape and size, what goes on inside us every minute and what we are capable of. It's an amazing journey.

Human life is a biologically degradable, chance based opportunity, not sought proactively by any one, I mean a request to be born…has never happened …did it ?

It's a marvelous system of sensory perception and emotions; its response mechanism is incomparable, indomitable and impeccable. The replenishing and rejuvenating systems are unparalleled. It's unfathomable in its capacity and capabilities; it's limitless in spirit and imagination.

To state simply, 'Life is a great chance'. A chance that had many possibilities of not making it to life, at every stage of growth from a single cell to who you were yesterday, today and tomorrow. There are no stakes to lose.

I thought of running you through some fascinating & very simple facts in life. You know them. It's just an attempt to remind.

Fact-1 :   'You' have not chosen your life.

Fact-2 :   'You' are not the one who created it either.

Fact-3:   'You' had no choice of gender / parents / nationality / species among many other choices.

Fact-4:   'You' had equal chances of making it to the world and not making it.

Fact-5:   'You' don't have control over many factors related to your internal physical and mental growth, as you were born.

Fact-6:   'You' don't have control over external interferences in our life, like nature, some diseases and untimely death, at any time in your life.

Fact-7:   'You' have come into this world with zero beliefs, responsibilities, rights, material wealth, fame or success. All are created right here.

Fact-8:   'You' will die one day and that's certain, you have very less or no control over it.

Fact-9:   'You' will when you die, take nothing with you, neither your beliefs, values, attitude nor your material possessions.

Fact-10:   Going by the above, you have nothing to lose at any point of time in your life. A zero sum game.

The Miracle - 'You'

"You only have to do a very few things right in your life, so long as you don't do too many things wrong."

- Warren Buffett

The life we fear, complain, drag, misuse, limit is a miracle in all its forms. 'The facts of life' clearly established that we are in possession of this miracle and living it, even without wanting it or creating it.

We are living an enriching, valuable, highly sophisticated, life of an advanced species in comparison to many other species lower in the food chain, yet we complain and some of us on a daily basis, for tiny issues of trivialities in return to the gigantic opportunity we are endowed with. This is no philosophy but pure logic.

If rainbow, eclipse, oceans, volcanoes, earthquakes, tsunamis baffle us, amaze us and excite us with their complexity, uniqueness and mystique, so should the life we live on a daily basis, keep us enticed and excited. As it's no less a miracle than all the above mysterious astronomical and natural events.

The day we realize this, we will live this life to value it much more than the tiny obstacles it presents while walking this grand path of unlimited opportunity.

If life is made into a routine of hundred tasks in a day, and a grind for attaining just plain material goals, one fine day after spending 45 years of your life, you will wonder, what have I lived my life for? What did I do with my last 45 years? How did they fly? And let me assure you, the answers wouldn't be very calming and reassuring. Even if you ask these questions at whatever age you are at, it will shake your very foundation.

I believe every moment, is to relish the splendor of life. Every challenge, a great opportunity to showcase your capability and every obstacle to conquer with your insurmountable spirit, and then... where is failure?

My dear friend, failure will never bother you, no matter how big, as long as you are bigger. Macro Perspective works.

GOALS

Every day across the world, scores of men and women are 'giving in' to small and mighty obstacles. They are giving up goals, retracting on commitments, shaming themselves and others who are dependendent on them. Some are compromising on quality, respect, trust and standards and some are losing health, wealth, relationships and peace.

"Goals are a means to an end, not the ultimate purpose of our lives. They are simply a tool to concentrate our focus and move us in a direction. The only reason we really pursue goals is to cause ourselves to expand and grow. Achieving goals by themselves will never make us happy in the long term; it's who you become, as you overcome the obstacles necessary to achieve your goals, that can give you the deepest and most long-lasting sense of fulfillment."

- Anthony Robbins, One of the world's leading Life Coach

Families are shattered, relationships are broken, respect is lost, credibility is challenged, inconfidence rules, wealth beseeched, strength destroyed, options limited, professions fail, organizations fall, teams degrade, and countries collapse, these are some of the outcomes of a very long list of mismanaging goals, which impact people, professions, groups, communities, organizations and countries on a daily basis.

It's very important to understand goals with an effective perspective to realize them. The intricate relationship of the subject 'Managing Obstacles & Failures' with goals need not be heavily explained, as you very well know, we wouldn't be talking of obstacles and failures, if we don't have goals to accomplish.

I personally consider our goals are the bedrock of all obstacles & failures, we face in our life.

Lack of goals can lead to some obstacles and having goals can lead to few others. That way, you are never assured of not having obstacles in your life.

Analysis of Your Goals

"When you are nobody, you have nobody."

- Jagapathi Babu, Movie Actor

Most of the goals are naturally driven out of your Value list and Value priority as discussed in the first chapter. If your goals are not in congruence with your values, or your values are not in congruence with your goals, there is bound to be a 'Value Conflict'.

In general terms, you identify this scenario with different issues like, lack of job satisfaction, lack of motivation, and lack of morale, stress.

Value based goals are the closest you can get to balanced goals, despite all subjectivity embedded in the definition of a goal. In real terms, 'if your goals can support your values consistently, you have arrived'. Goal setting is that simple.

In my personal interaction for this book with Premchand Degra, the only Mr. Universe, in his height category that India has ever produced in the professional body building sport, I have figured some of his primary values are 'sharing' and 'relationships' not 'money' and 'fame'. No wonder he is not someone who endorses a hundred products and mints millions, despite the fact, he could have.

His current goals clearly depict his values and his values are completely supported by his goals. He charges Indian Rupees Rs.250/ per month in his gymnasium in Hoshiarpur in Punjab to help budding bodybuilders learn from him personally.

Imagine someone with his values; trying to set a grand goal of setting up a chain of premium gymnasiums across this country, he might face huge value conflicts in the process of reaching those goals. Today he feels very successful with his modest endeavors in his small town and is at peace with himself. Nothing to complain.

"My Success is in helping my students raise ranks and become national & international champions. "

- Premchand Degra, Professional Body Builder, Mr. Universe

Mr. Degra's goals are so selfless, that any larger commercial selfish motive to make money for him can create stress in him and relieve him of his current state of happiness. I hope you can connect this to the 'value conflict' we have discussed in Fundamentals.

At the same time, someone from the same fraternity can have a different set of values and there by different set of goals. Arnold Schwarzenegger for example, the unparalleled and undisputed king of professional body building with several Mr. Universe and Mr. Olympia titles has consistently proven to the world, how his values are, and how he supported them with his beliefs, which are more stronger and larger than those muscles he has built in his best body building days.

"The fulfillment I experience when I see happy shoppers outside our stores, when I see our shopping bags outnumber those of the competitors or when I see the simple smiles of pleasure on the faces of our customers, is far greater than any award I have got till date. My goals are very simple to measure."

- Kishore Biyani, Chairman, Future Group

His goals and values are in congruence at all times and no wonder the man today is an icon for 'thinking big' and achieved global goals in short spans. Imagine reaching 3 global goals in one life time, in completely different areas like sports, movies and politics.

The above examples clearly establish that 'most goals are effectively accomplished and the outcomes are cherished, if they are in congruence with ones' values.'

FOCUS

'Obstacles are those frightful things you see, when you take your eyes off your goal.'

"Focusing your life solely on making a buck shows a certain poverty of ambition. It asks too little of yourself. Because it's only when you hitch your wagon to something larger than yourself that you realize your true potential."

- Barack Obama, President, USA

I have recently bought a luxury salon, a Laura Limited Edition, by Skoda in pearl white color. It was my wife's choice, as she felt there were very few cars of that model and color in the city. The very next day after we bought, I was driving her around in the city, she starts counting the similar model cars and worse still, similar colored ones and I could sense, she was a little disappointed, as she found many.

"Focus is irreplaceable, while hunting large goals"

- Prof. Ram Mohan Rao, Dean, ISB

Infact this model and color cars were not picked up by others in the city, the same day to disappoint my wife, as you can figure it out. They were there, even before. It's simple that, she started focusing on that make and color car just from the day we owned it. On a lighter side the power of focus is that impactful. 'If you seek, you will find.'

In obstacle & failure management this 'driver' has a great role to play, as it's a decisive factor in effective management.

There could be instances where you encounter more obstacles or failures in a certain phase of your life, with increased focus on them. Sometimes the events and situations in life can compel us unconsciously to shift our orientation from positive to negative and start focusing on all the wrong areas which increases the probability of obstacles & failures. In either case, 'Focus' plays a crucial role.

Whatever you focus on, you are bound to find it. Not just once, but many times over. If your focus is on happiness, you will find it. If on sorrow, you will find it too. If it's on your goals, you are bound to attain them…and succeed.

The point I wish to make here is simple and very natural. It's proven that you attract and possess what you focus on. Those of us who are getting bogged down and overwhelmed by obstacles are actually somewhere, somehow drawing them towards us by focusing on them. And those of us who are less visited by obstacles and failures are most likely focusing somewhere else...on their goals.

Most of the issues with Goal management are connected with focus. Lack of focus on goals can lead to lack of planning for obstacles and lack of preparation to attain goals, lack of armor and arsenal both mentally and physically.

No wonder most of those who fail, are surprised at their failure, despite the fact the signs of failure were written all over the place for very long, and there were enough indicators and red flags. It's plain simple that many do not focus on these warnings before they actually encounter and experience large obstacles or failures.

I recommend 'Value Driven Focus' [VDF]. Focus which is driven through empowering values towards goals is very lethal and can empower you to reach your goals any day, despite any odds.

Individual Application

This driver needs to be examined and tested before you undertake Goal Setting Process [GSP] and goals need to be aligned to match your focus levels.

If you are prone to distractions and you are habitual in deviating from your goals, with your past record of the same, it's better you set smaller and realistic goals and not large and complex goals. You are bound to invite lot of obstacles, with your lack of focus.

If you are one of those individuals whose focus is impeccable, the GSP could be liberal and in congruence with your external environment of opportunities and internal skill sets and values.

I don't foresee any major hassles for you, even if you set large and grand goals. I am not assuring that you will not encounter obstacles , but your powerful driver 'Focus' can help reduce the number of obstacles and with your focus you can manage them effectively.

You can focus on an obstacle or a failure, if you are challenged by them on your way to reaching goals to effectively manage them. While the rest of all time, let your 'Focus' be, on 'Goals'.

Organizational Application

This driver has immense impact on organizational application too. It can be small, medium or even large business houses. Lack of focus on the organizational values can lead businesses into different directions with short term gains. The lack of 'Value driven focus' is why many organizations run into the rough weather as they struggle to get out of businesses, which they have entered to make a fast buck.

In my board level interventions, I insist that organizations understand this core effectiveness. Lack of focus not only affects the bottom line through mismanagement of capital flows but also crucial areas like HR, operations and research.

If you don't know where your organization is headed from now in another 10 years and if you cannot control its flow into other businesses with visionary, mature, value based strategic choices, you are preparing your organization for an onslaught of obstacles & failures.

I don't wish to talk too much on organizational obstacles & failures, as they are plenty to discuss and my exclusive 'Obstacles & Failure Management in Organizations' a one day seminar will address most of the issues as a part of my corporate training service for organizations, who are willing to regain focus on their value driven goals.

Questions on Focus

I want you to ask yourself few basic questions right now -

1. What is that one thing, I am focusing primarily in my life right now?

2. How much time, am I spending on it, feeling, thinking & acting?

3. What kind of results I am getting & what am I doing with those results?

4. How long should I keep focusing on this aspect?

5. How many more areas, am I focusing on currently?

The answers for the above questions can lead you to understand the impact of focus and the disasters that hound you with lack of it.

There's a possibility that you can be in a situation sometimes in your life, where too many areas demand your focus at the same time and test your capability to focus.

Not focusing on the 'important areas' till they become 'urgent' can lead to a scenario where you might have to handle many 'urgent' issues, which gets piled up over a period of time. You were probably not focusing on basics on daily basis; it ended up creating a reservoir of 'Need your focus now' items.

Similarly, such compelling multiple areas demanding your focus can play havoc with your Goals and dilute your focus. I was able to learn very quickly that 'multi tasking'; while managing goals can most of the time back fire.

If you wish to reach large goals, there are no short cuts. You cannot shoot into a group; you have to shoot at the target, point blank.

Arnold Schwarzenegger comes across as a text book example and ideal role model for 'Focus'. I urge you read his biography to get inspired further in this area. You can look at any phase of Arnold's life and you find him focusing on one large goal at a time, the way it's practically impossible for many to practice.

From body building to acting and politics, 3 global goals is not a simple matter to consider as sheer coincidence. It is scientific, and the immaculate power of 'Value Based Focus', which always works for him. The accumulation and spending of all your resources in one direction to reach one major goal at a time. It's amazing to see how this dedication attracts the success, no matter how many obstacles and failures may come by on the path.

However, focusing on one goal does not necessarily mean you are neglecting other areas of your life, it simply means that you are giving the highest priority to the one on hand.

Value Driven Focus

'What do I need to focus on?' and 'How do I get that focus?' are two crucial questions to reach goals. 'One prioritized goal at a time' can be the first answer and 'Resourceful Attitude' can be the other. Focus on both these areas is very important.

When people quote the clichéd 'Money alone cannot make one happy', I feel, it's applicable here. If my focus is only on a goal 'to make money' but not on, how I continue to make money, you will not be able to focus on the next important areas like Health, Family or Relationships.

The focus need to be both on the Goal and the driver of that goal - usually the values. The Value Driven Focus is the key.

Watch out for feedback on your focus

There will be a lot of feedback on your focus, from your immediate environment and of course the results. Actually the results can be a huge measure of where your focus is.

But some time, your family, colleagues, and friends will be able to tell you where your focus is and that can act as a good feedback to work on your Focus.

Company you keep

If you wish to focus on the effective areas of your life to reach large goals and to reduce or overcome obstacles, you need to check what kind of company you keep on a regular basis. If you are surrounded by a bunch of self righteous peanut heads, who are pessimistic and egotists, you can be very certain that your focus is in the direction of your doom.

As social conditioning is a scientific reality in altering our behaviors, you are better off with a group of individuals whose focus is in the direction of adding value than diminishing it. It's great, if you have common goals or even some common values.

There's a huge need to review your circle of friends and companions with whom you are spending more time, as there's a huge possibility of you unknowingly slipping into stereo types. Their focus can yet times become yours, you will never know.

You might have realized how important this driver is. We have spent ample time here.

COURAGE

"Courage is not the absence of fear, but rather the judgement that something else is more important than fear."

- Ambrose Redmoon, Philosopher

No passion robs so effectively the mind of all its powers of acting and reasoning, as fear.

In the course of my research and profiling successful obstacle managers, I found, there is one key commonality in almost all the effective obstacle managers 'courage'.

You can imagine, the lack of courage can turn almost anything into an 'obstacle' for an individual.

Being endowed with this driver can increase your capability to encounter experience and overcome obstacles. In fact, mere possession of this driver can reduce the number of obstacles on your way. This driver is a critical component to driving obstacles at you and helping you manage the same.

"All our dreams can come true, if we have the courage to pursue them."

- Walt Disney

Courage necessarily need not be the dramatic expression of valor, strength or power but the simple capability to look into the eye of an obstacle or a failure and have the composure to not be scared and a will to overcome it, to progress towards effective obstacle management.

If I attempt to objectively define empowering courage, it is "a consistent, balanced and rational response through accountable action, with sincere conviction and lack of fear of the consequence."

As quoted above, it's not just about 'lack of fear', but value driven response to rationalize the consequences of fearing the obstacle or failure keeping in view of one's goals.

When you are in the eye of the storm, the fear grips you like anyone else, but the one who gets out of it early to act fast with decisiveness to survive, lives to fight another day. That's Courage.

Courage as you can analyze is a weighed, methodical response of an emotionally balanced, mature and action oriented individual. The capability to overcome the emotions such as fear, uncertainty, loss, despair and replace them with hope, clarity and control.

Courage Implications

"You got to have courage. Need to be fit physically, mentally & spiritually to live and fight obstacles."

- Salman Khan, Movie Actor

Courage is one of the core components of Obstacle & Failure Management, without it, failure is certain.

It is the lack of courage which holds you back from making another attempt after experiencing failure. Those who give up the fight in between or abandon their goals on impact from obstacles and failure lack courage to continue on the chosen path.

Those who are used to beaten paths, lack creativity, willing to just follow, averse to risk taking, cannot invent, and those who do not fight to support their values lack this driver and in most cases end up attracting more obstacles & failure.

Most often than not, lack of courage is not incidental and situation specific. It's a prolonged conditioning affected on you from various quarters as you grow up to become an individual.

"I don't think I would have ever achieved what I did, if not for the courage to make decisions to steer my life, at every cross road of my life."

- Vijaya Rama Rao, Former CBI Director
& Former State Minister

Testing your 'courage quotient' can actually give you a measure of possible success in your life. There is hardly any success story without courage playing a major role.

- ❖ Fear of initiative

- ❖ Fear to express

- ❖ Fear to lead

- ❖ Fear to risk

- ❖ Fear of Goals

- ❖ Fear of failure

- ❖ Fear of Other's invalidation of your actions

- ❖ Fear of family

- ❖ Fear of the society

- ❖ Fear of your own incapability

- ❖ Fear of unpredictable results

- ❖ Fear of fraternity

- ❖ Fear of making new decisions

- ❖ Fear of taking new paths

- ❖ Fear of encountering obstacles

The above fears can take you away from your goals and curtain the courage to face obstacles. Courage can fabulously increase the probability to effectively manage obstacles & failures.

'Fear' by itself can be a huge obstacle to overcome. Any resistance to accountable action in the process experiencing obstacles can be termed as 'fear' and you better be very careful in not letting this feeling take over you, especially in the times of adversity. Most of the delays in action to overcome obstacles & failures are the result of lack of courage.

In my personal interaction with Mr.Prem Chand Degra, the professional body builder and the only Mr. Universe in his height category, I strongly felt this driver is the most crucial factor which led him to success.

A small town boy with no knowledge or the implication of the sport, which was not even considered a great sport at that time and without having a role model to look up to, Prem went on courageously to set the largest grand goal for himself, "I want to be Mr. Universe."

The entire global sports fraternity and specially from the professional body building domain were shockingly surprised to actually see this boy grow up in a span of 8 years to be Mr. Universe representing India.

Courage can be a very valuable driver to invest into, for effective Obstacle & Failure management. You need to transform it into 'Balanced Courage' to drive solutions for effectiveness. We will pay more focus on this driver in the later chapters, when you discuss the application of the same for Obstacle & Failure management.

ACTION

It's the fact that all the 5 drivers have great impact on creating obstacles by either the lack of them or being ineffective measure. They are also equally lethal to find solutions to overcoming obstacles by the application of the same effectively.

You will completely agree with me, if I say, lack of action in one's life can drive huge obstacles. It's a certainty. There's no doubt, that if you sit tight and do nothing, with a mindset that, 'if I don't do anything, I might attract less obstacles', I am certain that you will be proven wrong.

"My Actions drive results all the time. Sometimes they are desired and sometimes, they are not. But I recognize that I am a leader and need to consistently act for the cause I believe in, despite whatever results."

- K. Chandra Shekar Rao [KCR], President, TRS

But 'action' which is irresponsible, unplanned and uncalled for can also create obstacles and set oneself up to failure.

In my personal interaction with several individuals, who have faced miserable failures and have resurrected themselves by effectively overcoming the adversity, I could gather their most difficult times were the times of 'inaction', where they were stalled from any action.

Those times, when they felt completely helpless and out of control, times when they could not act on anything, when they had to just wait for things to get right, when they felt a vaccum in their life, until the day they started acting at least minimally to see the results flow.

One of the biggest blows you can experience on encountering a large obstacle or a failure is that 'incapacitation' experience. It stalls all action, that's the first step to hibernation. Some winners have confided to me, that hibernation could be one of the ways they might have managed some obstacles, which I personally don't encourage you to consider as an effective solution. Some action needs to be done at all times to over come adversity, any 'zero activity period' is not recommended.

"When I take action, I'm not going to fire a $2 million missile at a $10 empty tent and hit a camel in the butt. It's going to be decisive."

- George W Bush, Former President, USA

Regrouping, coping, reinventing, rejuvenating, restrategizing, rationalizing can be things you do to cope and retaliate on large obstacles or failures to effectively overcome. Mind you, all those terms have 'plenty of action' built into them, despite some might just be 'thinking activities'.

'Incapacitation to act' is the most dreaded and remembered period for all those who failed or face large obstacles. Most of those who had spent some time in this phase, felt worthless and it lowered their self respect, decision making, and confidence by further curtailing their will to act.

The longer you stay in this unresourceful state, the longer is your failure. The minute you start action towards overcoming, you are no more a failure. Action has the power to transform failure into success instantly.

Action Driven Obstacles

❖   Lack of Action - Lead to Obstacles & Failure.

❖   Lack of Goal Oriented Action - Lead to Obstacles & Failure.

❖   Irresponsible Action- Lead to Obstacles & Failure.

❖   Forced Action - Half baked results, no conviction, and Constricted growth.

❖   Emotional Actions - Uncontrolled Outcomes, Relationship disasters, mostly leading to obstacles & failures.

❖   Unstructured & Unsystematic Actions - Lead to Obstacles & Failure.

❖   Unplanned actions - Lead to Obstacles & Failure.

❖   Untimely Actions - Lead to obstacles & failure.

❖   Contemplation & Indecisive Actions - Lead to obstacles & Failure

❖   Action based on Presumptions & Misunderstanding - Lead to Obstacles & Failure

Accountable Action

"As long as Ideas do not transform into accountable action their worth is unassesable."

- Uday Wagrey, Entrepreneur

This can be a huge obstacle manager. The answer for all the need for action in your life is addressed by the term 'Accountable Action'. Its self explanatory, if your actions are in tune with your empowering values, empowering beliefs and driven out of resourceful attitude, it will be 'Accountable Action' and will have immense impact on your effectiveness to manage and overcome obstacles & failures.

I hope you have assimilated this chapter well. The five drivers, which are basis and cause for any type of obstacle and failure you face, are double edged.

Impoverish or disempowering drivers can only drive the Obstacles & Failures, while the empowered ones can drive solutions to empower you to overcome the same.

I don't need to highlight the need to focus on your drivers and transform them to support your journey towards your goals.

The arsenal and summit chapters in the book ahead will utilize these drivers to drive most of the solutions and measures for obstacle & failure management.

Model Explanation

The model showcases the cycle of drivers acting on the outcomes. All the 5 drivers are crucial for experiencing Success / Obstacles / Failure.

The flaws in any driver can cause damage to the outcomes and there by all the 5 drivers are equally important to be effective for a wholesome experience of success.

The simplicity of this model is, if you face any obstacle in any area of your life, you simply have to look at the five drivers and assess which driver or drivers are affecting you at that point of time. Correction is also that simple, as the drivers which are driving obstacles for you in that phase can be corrected with your intervention to drive solutions instead.

I consider pentagon model is very important to all individuals to visualize at all times, both in the times of adversity and in the times of great success.

"Some obstacles can be planned for, others occur unexpectedly. Certainly those that can be anticipated should be planned for. One should consider what the options will be for surmounting the obstacle should it occur, weigh those options, and then have a plan for pursuing the option that is deemed best."

- *Prof. Kathleen A. Krentler, Professor of Marketing, San Diego State University [SDSU]*

CORE UNDERSTANDING

CORE UNDERSTANDING

Defining Obstacles

"All the adversity I've had in my life, all my troubles and obstacles have strengthened me... You may not realize it when it happens, but a kick in the teeth may be the best thing in the world for you."

- Walt Disney

Obstacle, A word that makes an individual sit up and take notice. It can unsettle, scare and even compel one to 'give in' or 'give up'. A word so powerful, that it can stall any progress, unnerve the mighty , rattle the weak hearted, and play havoc with individuals, communities, organizations and even countries.

I don't think there's any one in the world, who can claim to have not experienced obstacles. It's true; this very word is universal in its experience. But the way we handle this experience is as different and as unique as an individual.

"Obstacles are tests and failure is report card"

- Prof. Arun Tiwari, Co Author 'Wings of Fire'

An obstacle for me might not be an obstacle for you and likewise your obstacles might not even look like one for me. There's plenty of subjectivity in defining obstacles and the process with which each of us overcome them. Yet, there are innumerable commonalities in both effective and ineffective methods of managing ones obstacles & failures. That's where this analysis can help immensely.

The definitions, models and processes are arrived after deep research and detailed analysis through observation, reading, and interacting with many real time winners cut across different functional areas and professions.

I have personally met over 100 exclusive winners, who are extremely popular in their professions either regionally, nationally or internationally. It can be in sports, medicine, education, politics, military, research, home management, art, and judiciary, legal, social, or spiritual areas, for gathering their perspectives on this subject for you.

Welcome to analyzing, understanding and even redefining 'Obstacle' with objectivity.

It's a fact that most popular and most revered leaders and hero's faced some devastating obstacles, in comparison to their less popular and less legendary counterparts in the past and present.

I have learnt that success is to be measured not so much by the position that one has reached in life as by the obstacles which he has overcome while trying to succeed.

The greatness of any individual is measured by self and others on his proven capability to withstand and overcome obstacles. I hope you will agree that history hardly ever made a hero out of a timid, stereotyped, regular, contemplating, next door neighbor.

In my analysis, it is vividly evident, the greatness of the hero's of the world, always rested in their capability to summit the insurmountable obstacles with courage and ease, that made it look easy for innumerable others to follow.

"Obstacles in life are like 'hurdles race', you have to ride over them. They are bound to be there on your way."

- Salman Khan, Movie Actor

As we proceed further, we will attempt to completely demystify the word 'Obstacle' and gain clarity over it.

As per the American Heritage Dictionary

Ob·sta·cle

'One that opposes, stands in the way of, or holds up progress.'

In reference to the above on a humorous note Stendhal quotes.

'The lover thinks more often of reaching his mistress than the husband, of guarding his wife; the prisoner thinks more often of escaping, than the galore of shutting his door; and so, whatever the obstacles may be, the lover and the prisoner ought to succeed.'

So, obstacle is interpreted through the dictionary as 'one that opposes' 'stands in the way of' and 'one that holds up progress'. Most of us do perceive the obstacles in the similar manner.

There lies the key. The great leaders seem to not buy this definition that easily. Looks very much like, their very personalized definitions of these terms 'obstacles' and 'failures' are the primary reasons for their victories over adversity. I will appreciate your keen attention as we progress from here.

I strongly believe almost all great leaders have redefined Obstacles & Failures, to suit them, than going with what is a universal definition. Thomas Alva Edison for example, has defined it as 'different outcome than expected', as he failed over 10,000 times in the process of inventing the incandescent bulb. He used to respond to his distracters that he never failed; his argument was that he was able to discover 10,000 different elements that do not work for incandescent bulb. Genius, isn't it?

"The premise of 'failing' and 'failure' are for two different set of people. One who gets back and begins again in spite of miseries faced will be called just 'failing'. Lying low and accepting defeat and shedding whatever value one had after a failing can easily be deemed as a 'Failure'."

- Mir Ranjan Negi, Former Captain, Indian Hockey

Did this definition work for him? You bet. If not, we wouldn't have seen the light of his invention. Helen Keller defined obstacle as 'challenge to find strength'. Ranjan Negi defines it simply as "An opportunity to look at life, in a different way than before."

In fact in Mr.Negi's case, his capability to manage obstacles effectively in his life by his 'redefinition' has helped him to choose better options than a compelling thought of a suicide, when he was in the thick of a great adversity in his life.

It could be Mahatma Gandhi whose non-violence system was challenged almost every day by the obstacles like disbelief, lack of power, long ordeal, unending struggle, intangible outcomes, but he kept on defining the obstacles as "Tests to check your values, patience and resolve".

It could be Martin Luther King, Nelson Mandela, Christopher Reeves, Barack Obama or Arnold Schwarzenegger, all of them as you can relate to have adopted definitions other than quoted from the dictionary. If they were to look at obstacles as some which are stalling their progress, their strength to handle those obstacles would have reduced day by day. They most likely looked at the obstacles, as the temporary impediments and challenges to find alternate routes to get to their goals.

"If you're trying to achieve, there will be roadblocks. I've had them; everybody has had them. But obstacles don't have to stop you. If you run into a wall, don't turn around and give up. Figure out how to climb it, go through it, or work around it."

- Micheal Jordan, International Basket Ball Champion

Even today, many successful managers of obstacles & failures have and forever continue to redefine these words into what suits them best to move ahead towards the direction of their goals.

Real obstacles don't take you around in circles. They can be overcome. Invented ones are like a maze.

At this point, it will be quite appropriate to define not just obstacles, but also failure and success. As all of them are very intricately connected and are impacted by each other.

Let's define 'obstacle' objectively to suit most of your needs and especially for this book to help you.

Redefining Obstacle

"I feel the biggest obstacle is 'Death', anything else can be worked."

- Jagapathi Babu, Movie Actor

"Obstacle is a temporary, perceptive belief which challenges, hinders, slows down, subverts or delays the process of effective utilization of one's internal & external resources for effective and efficient outcomes."

In the chapters ahead, we will discuss in detail the process of obstacle experience, types of obstacles, degree of obstacles and the impact of them on various internal factors influencing failure & success.

Defining Failure

Imagine a day from your past, when you have failed at something. It could be a test, a project deadline, a communication opportunity, or a relationship, how does it feel? Do you have great, fond memories of your failures? Do you keep thinking of these incidents of failure to motivate yourself every day?

Failure, once accepted seems to be the bitter truth of our life and I don't think anyone celebrates their failure. But most of us after passing through failure quote:

❖　　"That was a great learning for me."

❖　　"I wouldn't have been, who I am, if not for that failure"

❖　　"That failure. Changed my entire life."

❖　　"Failure is a stepping stone to success."

64

❖ "There's no better teacher in the world, than a failure."

❖ "Failure gives you an experience of a life time."

❖ "Once failed, twice shy."

❖ "Failure is the basis of all change in beliefs."

❖ "If not for failure, there is no success".

There are innumerable 'positive experiences' of men and women on experiencing failure, but all in 'retrospect'. These quotes are usually given by those, who overcome their obstacles and failure, and have come out either less damaged or unscathed.

"Failure is living without peace"

- Prof. Arun Tiwari, Co Author 'Wings of Fire'

You can never catch someone in the middle of a failure or consistently in failure and expect the above quotes. You won't get it. Their experiences are painful, disdainful, depriving, defeating, pathetic and mostly true.

However, I can share with you some quotes by those who were experiencing large obstacles and failures and these quotes are not in retrospect.

❖ "It drains energy & makes me weak from inside."

❖ "It immobilizes you & shocks your logic".

❖ "Failure questions all that you have stood for, all that you have done and in one stroke, you lose it all".

❖ "Failure is a nightmare and can make you dread every night after".

65

- ❖ "Failure distracts you from the goals you have set and disillusions your future".

- ❖ "Failure takes respect away from you and isolates you from others".

- ❖ " Failure decimates your confidence"

- ❖ "I am left alone, as I failed. Even my wife deserted me."

- ❖ "Failure has the capability to destroy any kind of relationship, yet times even parental and spousal"

- ❖ "I wish it does not occur to my enemy".

- ❖ "Failure can sink your ship forever".

- ❖ "It wrecks your life and questions your sheer existence."

These are some of the very painful answers; I have got from those who are experiencing and those who have accepted failure.

"Failure is, when I cannot overcome the known obstacles in the system to contribute my best to the people who elected me"

- Vijaya Rama Rao, Former CBI Director, Minister for State

Of course if you don't accept, it's never a failure and can be considered an obstacle and you can overcome it. But yet times, by accepting it and moving on, you could learn and not experience a similar failure too.

It's not that hard to imagine now, despite failure being a stumbling block and harrowing experience which no one wishes to encounter, once overcome successfully the amount of positive change that failure brings in individuals is evident for the quotes by those who have successfully overcome failures.

These men and women actually take time to review and analyze the impacts of failure in their life.

There are examples of many individuals who have traversed great phases in their life pretty confidently and somehow at one phase fallen into the trap of failure and subsequently get drawn into another from then on.

"I don't think failure exists just in your mind. In real it's a non-entity"

- Jagapathi Babu

I was listening to Mr.Huckabee, one of the early republican contenders in the presidential race for USA recently in an interview with Larry King, after his failure at the party primaries.

When asked by Larry about, what are his plans after his failure at Primaries? He was very prompt in saying "I never planned for failure; I was focused only at winning. I strongly believe if you focus on 'what if I fail', you are bound to be drawn into it. We are like rivers; we flow to where there is less resistance."

Despite Mr.Huckabee failing at his attempt to be the presidential front runner for the elections, his insights into what to focus on are very crucial for his future attempts at being President of USA some day.

Abraham Lincoln did not fight to finish in one election nor did many great leaders across the world. Most of them have tasted failure prior to the most acclaimed success.

At this point I try defining failure as I see it, and to help you through this book.

Redefining Failure

'Failure is letting an obstacle to permanently stall or subvert the process of reaching a certain goal and in due process reducing options. Least are the options, greater the failure.'

"I just cannot think of failure, maybe I did not ever experience that feeling or maybe I am too adamant to accept it"

- Mrs. Deepti Reddy, Managing Editor, WOW Magazine

If you pay attention to this definition, I want you to focus on 'letting' and 'reducing options', as they tend to transfer all the burden of failure onto you.

I strongly believe, majority of failures are manageable, when they were obstacles. Our conscious and unconscious slip of 'letting them' turn failures, is crucial. The process of attacking obstacles, before they turn into failure is about 'how to effectively manage obstacles & failures'.

The reason I advise you to hold yourself responsible for your failures is, to give room for correction to become better the next time around. That's what professionals do, isn't it, learn from their mistakes.

If you don't admit to one, how can you learn? Professionals learn to take the blame and find the most effective solutions possible to convert the obstacles to success than failure.

The real failure is not about others recognizing you as a failure. It's when you recognize yourself as failure; you actually experience the failure in its true essence.

It's likely that most of the failures can just be branded as 'unlucky', 'destiny',' wronged by others', 'at the receiving end', 'collateral damage , 'environmental issues' to find solace in excuses.

So, all the sweet talk of failure being a great fuel for success is only after a thorough lapse of the 'failure after affects' and while it's on, failure can play havoc with all your systems and processes in a way sometimes can cause irrepairable damage physically and mentally.

The objective of this book as shared with you earlier is to help individuals overcome obstacles, when they are still obstacles and make sure those are not turned into failure, by lack of efficient action.

Defining Success

"Success is a lousy teacher. It seduces smart people into thinking they can't lose."

- Bill Gates, Chairman, Microsoft

In one of the Rotary discussions I have attended in Thailand, this subject of Success came up and each of the Rotarian was trying to project his understanding of Success. At the end of it, I felt almost all the definitions of success are so correct, as they are projecting their very own definition of the term.

Success, it's very personally defined and is extremely subjective.

It's perfectly alright to define it to suit your needs. I will share with you, some of the definitions my fellow Rotarians felt about success:

❖   "Success is about the increased capability to give to the needy."

❖   "It is a higher level of social acceptance and respect"

❖   "It is vindication of one's professional prowess"

❖   "It's the outcome of hard work and dedication"

❖   " It's the financial capability, overriding all else"

❖   "It's the pride of reaching goals".

But one of my all time favourites is the definition by Coleman York, the country owner for DS Max in 90's in India, when I took up my first enterprising initiative in sales and marketing with then second largest direct marketing company in the world. He used to quote.

"Success is like tasting Champagne, taste it once and you will never want to, let go."

- Coleman York, Country Owner, DS Max India

Very gustatory sense driven, symbolic definition. In fact it drove me to taste the real champagne very early in life, literally.

Here and now I attempted to define, 'Success' in a way, that it can mean something to everyone. The idea is to dissolve the subjectivity as much. It's not an easy task. The definition should work to help individuals, measure their success not just externally or materially but by the actual emotion, as success is after all an 'emotion'.

This definition, I believe suits all inclusive, material and spiritual. Give it a good thought and you might be able to appreciate the depth and application ease.

Redefining Success

'To create, possess and increase options, through managing obstacles consistently to reach pre determined goals. Greater the options, higher the feeling of success.'

If you pay attention here to 'manage obstacles consistently', 'increasing options', 'reaching pre determined goals' are three primary components to success, which can be measured internally.

In my understanding all success is about having options.

Think about it. Even feelings of success will have more choices internally than failure. If I am successful, it means 'I have options'.

"Success to me is about attaining a certain sensibility that one finds within oneself. This sensibility is something I cannot measure or define. It is about a particular moment, an instance, an expression, an experience that is realized."

- Kishore Biyani, Chairman, Future Group

I hate to compare, but we do it all the time in the society we live in, so if you compare someone's success, it's actually the comparison of options, one has. He might not utilize those options, but still the one who is in possession of many options is the most successful.

On the Material Application

Warren Buffet does not live in an expensive mansion in Manhattan, he chose not to. Is he not successful, think about it? If you think of Warren Buffet, the wealthiest man in the world, you can imagine the number of choices the man has materially. Almost anything which can be bought, if he chooses he can own.

Mr. Warren Buffet or Mr. Bill Gates would for sure have more options to choose from, than you or me as they are more successful in the wealth front, the material comforts; they have almost infinite choices in comparison to that of mine.

"Failure is success, if we learn from it."

- Rtn.Ravi Vadlamani, Past District Governor, RI 3150

Some of the options whose answers don't need to be thought hard by them are, where to work, when to work, what to eat, where at, when to, with whom, how, what to buy, where, when, where to live, how, when, with whom, are some.

For most of us, who are not as materially wealthy and successful the above could be questions, whose answers need to be carefully and selectively chosen as we might not have that many options left, in any case.

Social Front

Even applying the definition to non material success, the greater the success, the greater the options to give. Again those who have more options are more successful in the social responsibility front. Options like intention, time, skills, energy, motivation etc.

Service Front

Mother Teresa would have never been recognized world over as a success story, if not for her innumerable options of service, she possessed.

Her choice of place, time, people and service. Her success is measured by the choice of services to 'select people' who deserved it across any part of the world.

She was not limited. She had unlimited options, she could choose. She was successful. Here again the definition is applicable.

Think about it, the definition can be made applicable to define success to suit everyone's need from a school going child to a monk in a monastery.

Conclusively, imagine the feeling of success. It liberates you, even an internal feeling of success, is about options. If you reverse it, it works too...Imagine having lot of options, you feel successful.

Everyday, when men and women struggle to wake up and drive to work to get their paycheck to pay their bills and to grow their children, the limiting options is what upsets them, it limits their aspirations for better life.

Better transport, better education for their children, better environment to live. I think the entire rat race, we are at in our entire life on a daily basis is to increase options in our life. A better home, better car, better pay, better social status etc...

'Success is about increasing options. More options more success.' I urge you to apply it to any area of life and see how it holds well.

Now What

Once we define this, success seems very easy to acquire. You just have to focus on increasing 'options' in all areas of your life.

I have discussed in the chapters ahead on SMART Goals, the ability to take smaller goals and accomplish them consistently, will inspire you to achieve more as you can experience success at every level and really see the amount of options increase in your life, at every step of your growth.

> *"Today, I have a personal mission. I know that I have come into existence to live, to learn and to leave behind a legacy. And if I can make some people come together to build an institution to be cherished by the generations to come, I would have achieved a goal."*
>
> *- Kishore Biyani, Chairman, Future Group*

DEMYSTIFY OBSTACLES

DEMYSTIFY OBSTACLES

You will find several patterns which are actually deep seated habits in your life, some of them could be your pattern of speech, style of reception, style of writing, pattern of comprehension, pattern of thinking, pattern of building and sustaining relationships and many such conditioned habits in eating, dressing, socializing etc..

Similarly, I could also find a vivid pattern in how you define what obstacles are, how you experience those obstacles and how you either overcome or surrender to these obstacles.

Long ago I found a pattern of action, actually inaction which was bringing forth certain obstacles repeatedly in my life. My failure to recognize it earlier did cost me quite a bit. The day I realized the pattern, streamlining my action and overcoming that set of obstacles was quite easy. I averted a disaster.

After years of my personal analysis through observations and experiences of my own and innumerable others across various professions and industry, I have realized that specific patterns exist, in a way one encounters and manages obstacle. I have also come to accept that these patterns can be recognized by us, if we are conscious and corrected before they can harm us.

"Feelings of jealousy, bossism and lack of tolerance are the key obstacles in any work place scenario and are bound to cause damaging obstacles for professional goals"

– Venki Mahadevan, Director Information Technology, Asia, Motorola, India

It is at times surprising and unsettling to see someone facing similar type and degree of obstacles several times over in a short period of time again and again, it can possibly mean, they are making same mistake over and over again. It also showcases their inability to recognize the pattern.

Characteristics of obstacles

Further to understanding patterns, there are some key characteristics of obstacles, these are unique to obstacles, and you will recognize the minute you encounter them.

An Obstacle -

❖   It can make you feel edgy, desperate, helpless and less powerful.

❖   It can create insecurities and lack of trust.

❖   It can drastically impact your confidence levels.

❖   It can question your beliefs and test your values.

❖   It can stir the emotions and unsettle thoughts.

❖   It can weigh heavy on your mind and impact your attitude ineffectively.

❖   It can affect your metabolism and play havoc with your physiology.

❖   It can disturb the flow of feelings, thoughts and actions and impact several dimensions of work, social and personal spheres.

❖   It can impact your value list, value sequence by either shifting the priority or at times completely decimating certain values.

❖   It can lower your options and at times make it seem like there are no options left.

❖   It can severely impact action and you can actually feel stalled.

❖   It can impact your rational thinking and highlight your weaknesses and vulnerabilities.

❖   It can be invisible and dormant at times and not even recognizable.

❖   It can slow down, subvert, stall or derail progress towards a goal.

I believe the magnitude and power of any obstacle is as big or as small as an individual who is experiencing it.

"I think greed can be the root cause of all obstacles."

— Jyothi Ashok, Home Maker

There are giants of men who have faced the wrath of a horrendous obstacle several times over in their life and yet, were neither overwhelmed nor incapacitated by them. And then there are those who on daily basis succumb, surrender and quit at the very instance of encountering even a tiny obstacle.

Whenever I hear somebody say 'life's hard', I am always tempted to ask 'compared to what?'.

What can be your obstacles?

"The only failure one should fear is, not clinging to the purpose they see as best."

- Dr. Jayaprakash Narayan, President, Loksatta Party

In my attempt to dig deeper to understand, what could possibly turn as obstacles for you, I found factors which are unimaginable to be construed as obstacles at times. In the process of explaining further, I will list out a few.

Think about it... what could possibly be your next obstacle? Most of us would like to believe obstacles are outside us and are caused by others or instigated by external situations. Obstacles are those scary, discouraging, daunting hurdles anyone would hate to encounter. But a focused attempt at it will fetch you the right answers.

The very purpose of this book and the title 'Summit Your Everest' is to highlight that most of the obstacles in life you face are the creatures of your internal factors. The drivers we have learnt, if you remember from the initial chapters. It's quite obvious that if you can 'Summit Your Everest' which is inside you, the external one is not that hard to Summit.

'Values' as obstacles

"I have a habit of neglecting obstacles while they are small. Eventually they turn into crises and I have to fire fight most of the time."

- Agam Rao, Entrepreneur & Educationist

Have you ever realized that your own values could be your obstacles? There are several individuals whose disempowering values can lead them towards several obstacles in their day to day life.

There are several others whose values are in conflict with other people while at work or at home or in the community they live. This conflict could present potential obstacles too.

For example, if you possess a disempowering value 'greed' as one of the top priorities in your 'value list', you are inviting potential obstacles, as most of the action or goals to support that disempowering value, will be driven to only acquire something personally for yourself. In the process pitting your self against many others, snatching their opportunities yet times.

Your everyday actions will be driven out of self centered, selfish acquisition motives and can potentially lead to conflict with others. And of course, you can never be a great team player, with the virtue of this value. Value conflict with this value is imminent and so are the obstacles.

Those individuals who are driven by any disempowering values to set their goals have more possibility to encounter obstacles and we can identify them as 'value driven obstacles'. Managing these obstacles isn't easy either as the values which are driving you, are disempowering ones. Most of the disempowered values can only create more Value Driven Obstacles [VDO].

"I have the habit of paying attention to obstacles at their infancy and I usually never let them grow beyond a size"

- K. Chandra Shekar Rao [KCR], President, TRS

Sometimes, even individuals with empowering values like 'service to humanity' do tend to draw obstacles. There are many exemplary men and women whose primary values are to bring in favorable changes for larger good of humanity. But the difference is that someone is fighting for empowering values and for a right cause, has more relevance, as its adding great value to numerous others.

So, it's perfectly alright to face obstacles to protect your empowering values, even if they might not be as grand as 'doing good to humanity', as long as they are adding value to you and others, even in a smaller sphere.

Empowering Value Driven Obstacles and Disempowering Value Driven Obstacles can be the terms used to differentiate them. [EVDO & DVDO]

Value composition [all those values which are in the value list and are important for you to support] can also drive potential obstacles to other people's value composition. For example, in the global issue of the religious terrorism 'the obstacles are driven by the distinctly different value composition of two groups...moderates and fanatics.'

Most of the conflicts at work place can be the result of either individual or team's value conflicts or the value conflicts between employee's value composition and organization's value composition.

Incessant obstacles such as miscommunication, lack of motivation, non alignment of goals, issues with delegation and resource mismanagement can result with organizational value conflict.

Beliefs as obstacles

"I have very strong beliefs, and I am aware that they are strongly founded."

- Kashif Suleman, Celebrity Martial Arts Expert & Actor

'I don't think it's achievable', has this belief ever achieved anything? It cannot. As beliefs such as this presents the pursuer of goals with more obstacles, while on their way to goals.

There are several such beliefs which we can term as 'Limiting Beliefs' [LB] and these beliefs can create potential obstacles.

Your beliefs are responsible for recognizing and as well as overcoming obstacles. Certain beliefs could themselves be obstacles. For example, 'hard work never pays' as a belief can possibly be one of the biggest obstacle for you to reach goals.

Most of the obstacles at work, family and community are also the result of belief conflicts. 'I know it works' and 'I know, it doesn't work' in a team are conflicting beliefs. This could potentially lead to obstacles in the way for the team, to reach its project goals.

Almost all obstacles and failures in one's life are driven out of beliefs and infact most of the external obstacles are the result of the internal interpretation of these beliefs. Overcoming these internal limiting beliefs is the biggest challenge to overcome the external obstacles.

Habits as obstacles

"Some habits do become so strongly conditioned that, even if you wish to get rid of them, you cannot."

— Jagapati Babu, Movie Actor

Your habits can potentially become obstacles for you and others. This factor is several notches complex and hard to overcome unlike several other internal obstacles.

Yes, some of your habits can be your obstacles, unless you transform them or get rid of them. Repetitive actions lead to habits and consistent satisfaction of habits lead to 'conditioning'.

'Conditioned habits' over years in one's life can be either assets or liabilities. Most of the liabilities lead to obstacles. I request you to pay attention to some major habits you can identify with yourself and check for their degree of conditioning, alongside check if they are assets or liabilities.

You will realize most of your habits which are 'liabilities' are in the driver seat of the obstacles you're either facing now, experienced in the past or bound to encounter in the near future.

There are instances where, with a change of one single habit, several obstacles can be surmounted at once and there are times when several habits need to be reconditioned to surmount one large obstacle.

"My habit of clearly expressing 'what I feel is right', caused several obstacles for me, but has lead me to fulfilling my obligations as the chief of army and later as the Governor for Jammu & Kashmir."

— Gen. K.V.Krishna Rao, Former Chief of Indian Army &
Governor for Jammu & Kashmir

'Disempowering Habits' are a cause for great concern and you need to be aware of the list of your [DH].

I have known many individuals who have missed great opportunities and have faced serious obstacles with their disempowering habits. A habit such as 'micro detailing'... meaning paying attention to only small details so much that most of the time you are focused at tiny issues, could lead to someone 'strutting small stuff' all along his life, and in the process missing out on larger picture and big opportunities.

There are several instances of DH's setting up obstacles for you, I have listed few habits, it could be as basic as your undisciplined lifestyle, habit of over eating, habit of over communicating, habit of exaggeration, habit of substance abuse, habit of complaining, whining, blaming others for your mistakes, habit of contemplation, habit of instant gratification, habit of rumor spreading, habit of bitching about others, habit of over indulgence, habit of wrong prioritizing, habit of sleep, habit of time sense, the list is long... most of these habits, you are aware are potential drivers of obstacles in your life.

Self discipline is one of the key parameters to check your efficiency in enabling 'empowering habits'. The capability to streamline and manage one's habits could eventually lead to effective obstacle management.

Emotions as obstacles

"It was the feeling of challenge which drove me to win the dream championship of Mr. India"

- Adhikari, Mr. India, Professional Body Builder

Being the core of all human activity, emotions play a key role as either being obstacles themselves or by empowering or disempowering individuals to manage obstacles effectively. Your own emotions can turn into obstacles for you.

Give it a thought...can fear be the one, feeling of desperation, feeling of superiority, feeling of inconfidence, feeling of inhibition, feeling of depravity, feeling of failure and many such emotions can potentially be obstacles for you. These emotions can be 'Disempowering Emotions'. DE's take power away from you, as they seem to destroy resources.

'Empowering emotions' like feeling of hope, feeling of confidence, feeling of pride, feeling of self respect, feeling of courage, feeling of challenge, and feeling of success can support you to surmount largest of the obstacles.

"I think it's the feeling of pride to represent one's country, which drives sportsmen to give their best, optimum utilization of their internal potential. Minus that feeling and they might fall short.

– Prof.Adrian Kennedy, Managing Director, Wellness RX Appollo

Almost all obstacles invoke emotions and they could be either empowering or disempowering. If you can focus on evaluating the type and degree of emotions which obstacles arouse in you, you will have a better chance to manage and overcome obstacles.

"Lack of trust worthiness and loyalty in spousal relationship can cause a lot of heart burn and communication obstacles for emotionally sensitive spouse in a relationship."

– Mrs.Pratibha Sagar, Home Maker & Director, Matrix Mentoring

'Emotional conflict' could be another trigger for obstacles, as set of your emotions can be on a collision path with that of others. There are several cases wherein your emotions are in conflict with others and can cause obstacles. Failing teams in professional projects, sports, social activities are examples of emotional conflict within teams.

"Consistent emotional exaggeration can create devastating obstacles in relationships and I find this trend is on an increase in spousal & work relationships."

– Mrs. Savita Date Menon, Clinical Psychologist

Obstacles in one's personal and professional life through emotions such as 'feeling of suspicion', 'feeling of being cheated', 'feeling of taken for granted', 'feeling of disrespect', 'feeling of intrusion', 'feeling of lack of privacy', 'feeling of suffocation' and 'feelings of threat, insecurity, jealousy' are crucial to focus on.

Exaggeration of one's feelings or suppression of feelings both can equally lead to obstacles too and impact professional, personal, social relationship areas.

Listing out all those emotions which could potentially be obstacles in your personal, professional and social life can help you, to be guarded.

Thoughts as Obstacles

'Idle mind is a devil's workshop' an old adage has relevance in this context. Most of the time our very own thoughts can be obstacles, especially when the mind is not in a resourceful state.

"The thoughts of my incapability to speak fluently in English haunt me even at nights. This is my biggest hindrance in life."

– Ms. Poornima, Young IT professional

Emotions drive thoughts and thoughts propel actions as you are already aware by now. Disempowering emotions mostly result in 'disempowering thoughts', leading to creating hurdles, hindrances and obstacles.

Obstacles which usually delay progress by means of contemplation, postponement of certain actions, and the flow of attaining one's goal are usually affected by defeating or disempowering thoughts. 'I think it will not fetch me results', 'I think there is a luck factor', 'I think there is more than what is obvious', 'I think I need to delay this decision ', are certain thoughts driven out of disempowering emotions and can truly be potential obstacles.

"Certain defeating thoughts always rattle in my mind and confuse me, they work against my confidence."

– Manoj Kumar, MBA, Management Trainee

'Racing thoughts' which are inconsistent and fluid can cause damaging obstacles through fostering inconsistency and unpredictable personality. Thoughts which are shrouded with suspicion, insecurity, lack of trust and deception can lead to actions which are compelling and break professional, social and personal relationships.

'Unmanageable thoughts' are what one need to be cautious about to avoid them to turn obstacles.

Great thinkers like Socrates have found solutions for seemingly insurmountable obstacles through their mature, definitive and visionary analytical thought process.

Listing out thoughts which affect you negatively and deemed to cause obstacles to your progress can help one continuously overcome obstacles and failure.

Actions as Obstacles

"I sometimes feel, I act a little overboard, while with a group. I sometimes end up talking more than needed."

– V. Agam Rao, Entrepreneur & Educationist

Most of the obstacles in one's life are the results of action towards accomplishing goals. However, it doesn't mean that inaction will not result in obstacles. In this context, inaction is considered as an action in the form of a decision, 'to not act' and thereby resulting in obstacles.

Actions as 'action with vengeance', 'action without logic', 'action untimely', 'delayed actions', 'hasty actions', 'actions without consequential analysis', 'action with prejudice', 'action without objective', 'self destructive actions' are some examples.

Individuals oblivious of the power of action end up either in 'inaction' or 'reactive action' leading to obstacles and failures.

'A stitch in time saves nine' a quote which haunts me to act without delay especially in the areas of relationship building and persuasion helped me personally to avert and manage several obstacles and failures.

I realized as individuals grow in age, there is certain amount of trial and error experience as learning in reference to 'action and its impact'. However it's not true for everyone.

Action's imperative in conditioning habits and eventually impacting obstacles and failures is a key parameter to assess one's action efficiency.

Congruence is the key in determining one's action capability. 'Accountable Action' is one that synergizes empowering values, beliefs, thoughts and habits towards effective and remedial action with immense congruence to overcome obstacles and failures.

'Incongruent Action' can create many obstacles and you need to be cautious of callous action, which can lead to professional, personal, social, and relationship obstacles.

Orientation as Obstacle

Have you ever noticed individuals who would turn cynical at every opportunity presuming and prejudging individuals and situations according to their preprogrammed judgments? There are some who could be critical, some who could be prejudiced, some who could be suspicious and some who would not trust, and some a combination of all the above, the reason for this biased judgment can be an 'orientation issue'.

"I fail to understand, why few people always try to twist facts and misunderstand most of the time, it's not incidental. It's almost regular."

- Ms. Poornima Hariharan, Entrepreneur

The systematic conditioning of certain set of values, beliefs, emotions, thoughts and actions which are wrongly led by ineffective role models can lead to 'orientation problems'.

The repetitive and consistent behavioral pattern in reaction to situation and events result in 'conditioned orientation'. In simple words, Chronic Liars, Bitter Critics, Extreme Suspects, Untrustworthy individuals, who will doubt every area of other's life, are bound to set great obstacles for themselves and others.

"One needs both emotional and intellectual strength to learn from the failures, to get out of them and to go ahead with success with revised plans of action."

— Dr. Y.S.Rajan, Principal Advisor,
CII & Co Author of 'Vision 2020' with Dr. A.P.J.Kalam

Those individuals who possess conditioned negative orientation can possibly encounter more obstacles in comparison to their positive cousins. The orientation, with which they express their entire behavior, is heavily impacted by the way they encounter and manage obstacles and failures.

I have personally known individuals with whom any amount of caution from your end to avert a misunderstanding will not work. They tend to find any verbal or non verbal cue to find faults or misunderstand communication. It never ceases to amaze me as to how they can successfully turn any positive situation into a negative one.

On a more serious note, individuals with negative orientation not only set themselves up for more obstacles and failures in their life but also become an obstacle for others at work, home and community.

The issues with orientation can be checked by effectively managing the feedback one gets from the environment around their home, work and community. Mostly 'ineffective orientation' presents one with social, relationship and communication obstacles.

Attitude as an Obstacle

The fertility of your thoughts is quite dependent on the soil over which you sow the seeds. The soil is 'Attitude'.

Your state of mind at any point of time determines your attitude and it subsequently determines the kind of thoughts you could generate.

"It's the sheer attitude of the winner, which makes him win & the loser to lose."

> - Dr. Kondal Rao, Former Director Telugu Academy &
> Chairman, Sister Nivedita Foundation

Empowering thoughts can generate only in a 'Resourceful State'. The state of mind which can become your obstacle is an 'Unresourceful State'[URS]. This URS can be a huge obstacle in one's path to success. It can also be an obstacle for others in relationships with you. It's very important to regularly collect feedback and manage the same through making changes to your attitude to steer clear of obstacles.

Your attitude has the power to either catalyze or deprive you of all success in reaching goals. It has the capacity to turn adversity into opportunity and an opportunity into adversity. All perception is the outcome of your attitude and perception is a very critical tool to effectively manage obstacles and failures.

No wonder one's attitude can spell glory or doom for an individual. It is also important for organizations to monitor employee attitude, families to focus on member's attitude and stake holder's attitude in a community. As all the obstacles faced by the above units are primarily because of the attitude of the members of these units.

Family, religious, educational and social conditioning results in 'Attitude Polarization'. It means, either you are conditioned internally to be in a resourceful state most of the time, which leads to 'effective polarization', which can help you with greater coping mechanism and reater problem solving capability or either 'ineffective polarization' which can lead to 'lower threshold limits' leading to serious problems in encountering, accepting obstacles and failures and obviously in managing the same.

Knowledge as an Obstacle

"Real knowledge is to know the extent of one's ignorance."

- Confucius

It's quite unsettling to know that even knowledge can set up obstacles, if one's not cautious about its application.

Yes, it's true and you might have experienced it several times, unconsciously. Very few people in my interaction have raised this subject; knowledge can, if mismanaged be one of the potential obstacles in your life.

"I believe knowledge if not managed effectively can transform into a major obstacle, locking one's potential to grow beyond."

- Prof.Ram Mohan Rao, Dean, Indian School of Business [ISB]

The mother of all obstacles for creativity is stereotyped, conventional, knowledge. 'I did it, because I was not aware that I couldn't', is what many inventors and discoverers wondered after their outcomes. Knowledge can either constrict you or free you, depending on how you apply it in your daily life.

Knowledge when not acted upon with congruence and application veracity can also become an obstacle for progress.

It is surprising that our nation which is one of the oldest civilizations on earth has very less role to play in the area of scientific inventions and discoveries, especially in the recent times. There were few names in the past, but it's fast receding, there are hardly any in the last several decades.

The biggest obstacle, as I can see is the system of education 'knowledge dissemination system', which acts as an end by itself than a means for an end.

The lack of challenge, question, enquiry, breaking norms in the tight boxes of knowledge dissemination, one is framed into succumbing, which subsequently results in a close mind, memory based knowledge and less inquiry driven knowledge application in real time. No wonder, our education at times can even be an obstacle to ascend to higher grounds of knowledge.

'Enquiry Driven Knowledge' can be a liberating factor, which can find solutions at every juncture and support you to manage obstacles and failures. 'Knowledge Trap' is what one needs to be cautious of, as it can cause many obstacles on your way. Especially professional, social and relationship obstacles can be driven out of mismanaged knowledge.

"It's the large urban educated elite, who do not utilize their vote, which franchises the wrong people to power in India. They have the knowledge of what is wrong, but they don't act to set it right."

— Dr. Jayaprakash Narayan, President, Loksatta Party

The reluctance to learn further, lack of reception to others point of view, intolerance to alternate schools of thought, lack of admiration for adventure, and to experiment is the result of knowledge being an obstacle in certain scenarios.

Lack of growth in one's profession or enterprise, relationship failures, respect and identity issues in family and community, repetitive mistakes and continuous failures, showcase one's incapability to use knowledge to cope, manage and overcome obstacles and failures.

For my fast growing 4 year old son Sahas, I and my wife Pratibha have coined a term 'ALPD' [Average Learning Per Day]. It's self explanatory.

I felt, it can be applicable to me and you too. If I can keep track of what I am learning in a day and how am I using that knowledge, it can greatly help liberate knowledge for its effective application. It pays to have 'knowledge' on your side, than 'fight' it, right!

Goals as Obstacles

Though it may seem like goals are external, I am of the view that real goals are very much internal and driven from deep within. As much as I have analyzed goals, they seem to be directly connected to one's values, supported by beliefs, affecting emotions, catalyzing thoughts and compelling actions, as we have discussed in the earlier chapters.

"The productivity of a work group seems to depend on how the group members see their own goals in relation to the goals of the organization."

— Ken Blanchard, Leadership Consultant & Author

Your goals can be your obstacles. If your goal setting process (GSP) is unscientific and is driven by disempowering fundamentals and ineffective drivers. If your goals are not objective, original, well thought of, skill and knowledge centric, compatible and SMART, then you are in trouble my friend. Your obstacles start right from your own Goals.

Goals can be obstacles in two distinctive scenarios

One is by not having a worthy grand goal to drive you and encourage you to overcome obstacles through different phases of your life. And another is to have a gigantic and unscientifically set BHAG. [Big Hairy Audacious Goal].

You will agree, your GSP can lead you to set goals and if they are set unscientifically and callously, they can later in your life become big obstacles, not just for you but to everyone associated with you. You can be aware and cautious of this 'Faulty GSP', which can be the cause.

There are several individuals who, without purpose wander through their lives with no worthy goals to accomplish. They tend to face many obstacles, especially in their later years of life, when either finances or relationships can drive obstacles for their lack of goals.

There are some who are occupied all day, all night, all life for accomplishing their goals which they never seem to reach. As their goals are highly unrealistic, unscientific and too large to feel accomplished, these individuals face loads of obstacles and at times fatal failures.

In the organizational perspective, leaders and mangers who cannot set SMART goals can lead teams to obstacles through 'Faulty GSP' resulting in less morale, inconfidence, lack of challenge and job satisfaction, eventually leading to high levels of attrition.

Yes, your Goals can be obstacles, if not set up and pursued well.

Classification of Obstacles

Almost all the obstacles in your life can be classified under Personal / Family / Social / Global and Spiritual. And each of these obstacles can further be narrowly classified as emotional, financial, and relationship obstacles.

Model Explanation

Gradation of Obstacles - Degree & Size

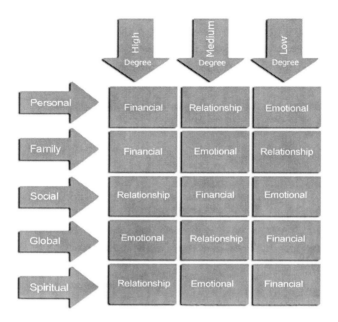

When individuals complain of how large their obstacles are they are actually referring to the size and degree of obstacles.

Obstacles do differ in size and degree

Some obstacles are small, some are big and some enormous. Some have smaller impact; some have medium and some devastating to those who experience it. No wonder few, even give up their life in the process of encountering, experiencing obstacles and failures.

Perception does play an important role in assessing the actual size and degree of an obstacle by you, as this assessment can be very subjective. For the ease of use in this book, my plan is to demystify the intricate factors, which affect the size and degree of an obstacle generally.

If a value conflict results in an obstacle, especially of your primary value set, the degree and size of the resultant obstacles can be expected to be large and the impact larger. Subsequently overcoming these obstacles can give you satisfaction and feeling of Success.

Similarly, the lower order value conflicts or belief conflicts can lead to medium or smaller obstacles and failures. The impact is less and short duration. The feelings of overcoming these obstacles will also be 'not very great'.

There can be many examples I can draw for the higher degree and lower degree obstacles. A traffic congestion , which holds you back while you are returning from office to home can be a smaller degree obstacle, the impact is irritability and discomfort for short duration and when you overcome this obstacle and reach home, I am certain you will not throw a party and celebrate the success. It's just a smaller degree success.

In contrast, if the same scenario is slightly altered and you are stuck in traffic congestion and your only child is in the ambulance with a medical emergency, the same obstacle can become a higher degree one and the impact is huge especially if the congestion continues for a longer time.

If you overcome this obstacle to reach the hospital eventually and get the needed medical attention and your son returns home healthy and hale after few days, the success of course is large enough to celebrate. It's a higher order success, as it is connected to your primary value 'Relationships'.

In another scenario, if something wrong happens to the child in the ambulance, while still in the traffic congestion and after reaching the hospital doctor tells you, that you brought him late. Imagine the impact of this failure on you. It will be extremely large and devastating and will have very long term impact on your memory and emotions.

Despite all subjectivity we can define higher degree, medium degree and lower degree obstacles and failures. You can check your value list to see how, some obstacles can turn large for you and some small, while for someone else, the same might not be true.

The size is referred usually to the quantum of impact on you in many dimensions financial, personal, social, professional etc...and both degree and size of the obstacle impacts can be measured by their impact on memory and emotions too.

❖   Your quick action to resolve higher order obstacles is advisable and learning a lesson or two from all obstacles and failures is highly recommended.

Coping Stages

As the obstacles appear before you, there are several stages which usually one goes through to encounter the experience and eventually manage the same. It is not necessary that all of you go through this in a similar format, but this generalization helps in assessment of our state close to the real.

Almost all of us go through this stages naturally, but some cross these stages too fast, some too slow and some just right. The idea is to attain the 'just right' tag in the process of managing obstacles and failures.

This can help you to assess your current stage while encountering an obstacle and lets you figure out possible solutions to overcome.

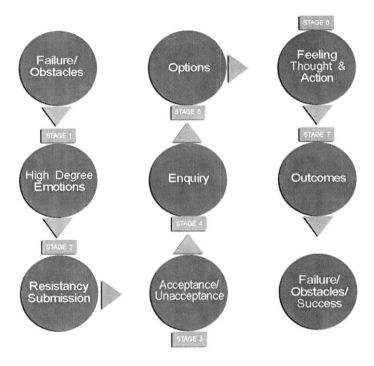

Most often than not the confusion that prevails in understanding the obstacle stages can hinder the analysis capability of an individual to ascertain the exact method to adopt for overcoming and resolving an obstacle or failure. Different stages might require different methods to overcome.

Identifying various stages can be of great help to initiate action to summit.

Stage 1

Realization

"Realizing that I have an obstacle is the first step to actually overcoming it."

- Ratna Rao Shekar, Editor, WOW Magazine

There is a huge possibility of experiencing higher degree emotions in this stage such as shock, disbelief and discomfort at the first encounter of an obstacle.

These emotions, if not given time to recede naturally can at times lead to individuals experiencing confusion or chaos. The best method is to let these feelings be expressed internally and be aware of them and remain calm through this stage, without initiating any action. It's very important that you don't act in this stage. Any action in this stage, will amount to reacting.

Delay any action by compelled emotions at this stage.

Stage 2

Resistance / Submission

This stage is about resisting or submitting yourself to an obstacle on the path to goal accomplishment. Both are very important, viable and can yield different results.

Those who submit quickly to any obstacle without much resistance, tend to invite more obstacles as their capability to overcome decreases with their habitual response to surrender to obstacles.

I want you to get it right, there is a difference between 'accepting' that there's an obstacle to surrendering to it. Accepting is alright. But those who surrender will not attempt to overcome the obstacle at hand, as they try finding either an excuse or blame others or quickly change path. This habit can end you up taking up goals and very frequently changing the course of reaching them as you detour for every obstacle instead of overcoming and treading the same path.

"The challenge and open mockery at the championships that an Indian can never win this height category, has instigated me to work double hard to win the title of Mr.Universe and prove them wrong."

– Premchand Degra, Mr. Universe, Professional Body Builder

But in some critical scenarios where your resource capability completely limits your resistance, you can surrender and call it quits; it can be a smart move.

This situation occurs several times, when your Goal Setting Process [GSP] is faulty, you might have to surrender to your obstacles and failure at every juncture when your goals are challenged. No wonder those with BHAG's [Big Hairy Audacious Goals] which are unscientifically set eventually have to surrender to the consistent obstacles and failures they are bound to encounter.

I personally will not advise you to practice this surrendering as it can breed an ineffective habit of 'quitting'.

Those who surrender easily to an obstacle and give reasons of 'destiny' or any other unscientific terms are also exhibiting the lack of strength to fight and overcome an obstacle.

'Resistance' at this stage is also another possibility, and most of the leaders whose goals are driven from their primary value list and their GSP is scientific and SMART, stick to their goals and resist all the obstacles on their way to progress.

If you don't resist to the obstacles, how will you ever overcome them? Finding solutions to overcome an obstacle can only get initiated by one's resistance to quit on facing an obstacle. 'I will fight to win', 'There is no obstacle which can stop me from progressing' are some of the internalized beliefs most successful winners deploy to resist in this stage.

Stage 3

Acceptance / Unacceptance

"I don't think you can wish away your obstacles; they have to be faced boldly and overcome methodically."

– Prof. Arun Tiwari, Co Author 'Wings of Fire'

It is very natural to have obstacles on the way to goals. There is nothing to worry about it. Actually you should be more worried, if there are none on your way to your goal. May be you are not going towards a worthy goal.

Accepting and recognizing the obstacle, if it is truly present will allow you to act early to overcome it, than trying to lie that you have none. There are few people, who feel it's wrong to have obstacles in their way, and they would like to not just hide it from others but also lie to themselves. It does not help much.

"By wishing that there are no obstacles on my way and they will eventually disappear, I tend to sometimes not focus on managing obstacles as they appear. This tendency did present me with large fires to put out several times in my life."

— V. Agam Rao, Education Entrepreneur

Courage is all about acceptance of an obstacle on an encounter and initiating an early search for solutions. That's how any obstacle can be overcome. The delay in obstacle management most of the time, lies in this stage.

Many do not recognize obstacles and thereby do not accept them. Precious time to act is lost and the 'obstacle' presents itself a little later as a 'crisis' and can eventually turn into a failure.

Lack of courage, plain ignorance or manipulation leads to unacceptance and morphing the obstacle to your own self or to others. It delays 'solution search' as one feels incapable to find resources to overcome immediately. In this case, action comes too slow and can cause great damage.

Overconfidence, can at times lead you to not accept the obstacle on your path and in the process of displaying your strength and power, you might neglect the same. The implications of unacceptance of existence of obstacles can lead to delayed actions resulting in obstacles growing in size, degree and causing at times irrepairable damage to your goals.

Stage 4

Enquiry

"There's no end to the solutions one can find, if one persistently seeks powerful outcomes. If you don't ask, you don' get."

— Kingshuk Nag, Resident Editor, Times of India

This stage is about finding effective solutions to accepted obstacles. The crucial point to note here is, you will never get to this stage if you don't accept the existence of an obstacle. You can sense the danger lurking in the stage 3.

In this stage you tend to ask questions. Depending on the quality of questions you ask, you will get the answers and it impacts your effectiveness in solving the problems at hand.

'Why me?', 'Why do I have to face obstacles all the time?', 'Why do I have hardships all along my life?' are some weak questions you can ask, which do not possibly give great solutions to overcome the obstacles. These are not powerful questions focused at solutions, rather driven out of depravity and self pity.

'What could possibly lead me to overcome this obstacle?', 'How can I act to reach my goals?', 'What past experiences can I bank on?', 'What did I learn from this obstacle?' are some effective questions which can lead you to find effective solutions to overcome. Powerful questions yield powerful answers.

Stage 5

Options

"There is nothing more important than building more options for you in the times of adversity, as the challenge is against the least options you possess as you struggle to overcome failure."

– Prof. Gale Naughton,
Dean, College of Business Administration, SDSU

This is a crucial stage to manage or mismanage. This stage is driven from the earlier stage and once powerful questions resulted in powerful answers, most of them will be options.

Those who succeed consistently in overcoming obstacles, have the capability to search and generate more options and choose the best out of them as effective solutions.

On the other hand, those who fail at generating more options can end up with very less options to act upon, and in turn their effectiveness is lowered.

Exercising one's choice to build more options which can enable solutions is the key to obstacle management. While not exercising one's choice to explore options and sticking to a minimal few, compel the individual to act within limits, and results in most of the delays in resolution of obstacles.

"At the end of the day, no one expects more of me than I expect of myself."

– Prof. Kathleen A. Krentler, Professor of Marketing,
San Diego State University, SDSU

Stage 6

FTA (Feelings, Thoughts and Actions)

"Multiple Senses need to be utilized to overcome obstacles, its ain't simple."

— Salman Khan, Movie Actor

This stage sets in motion feelings which are either very important to overcome obstacles or those emotions which prompt you to delay or quit.

Imagine a feeling of 'confidence', 'courage', 'aspiration' or 'desire to succeed' can do to overcome an obstacle in comparison to what 'fear', 'inconfidence', 'deprivation', 'self pity' and 'demotivation' can do.

As feelings drive thoughts, the first set of feelings quoted above will invariably drive effective thoughts, thereby effective actions to overcome. While the second set of thoughts will drive ineffective thoughts and actions leading to mismanagement.

The stage is very important as most who quit their long cherished goals or those who win despite all odds are driven primarily out of this stage. Emotions are the basis of all action and this stage is very important to drive effective or ineffective emotions.

Stage 7

Outcomes

The earlier stage had set in motion a canvas of feelings, thoughts and actions to drive results .This stage is about 'outcomes'.

In this stage all action performed will yield outcomes, and is up for evaluation to verify if the outcomes are in congruence with the results desired by you to overcome obstacles and failures.

This stage is crucial for not just assessing the outcomes and experiencing success or failure on overcoming an obstacle, but it is very important as it forms new beliefs and strengthens the existing ones.

"It is like an alarm clock which reminds you to refrain from certain actions. One may call it as lessons or learning from past .My Asian games debacle in 1982 still rankle my thoughts."
— Mir Ranjan Negi, Former Captain, Indian Hockey

If you were to effectively overcome an obstacle, this outcome will be registered as an experience, which will boost your confidence and strengthen all related beliefs and values, paving way for similar action in future.

In contrary, if your outcomes have ineffectively managed the obstacle and lead to a failure, the experience will strengthen beliefs related to 'inconfidence', 'inferiority' and will shift your value sequence.

It's very important, that you pay attention to how you are judging your outcomes and what measures you are adopting in this stage, to check if you are effective in generating effective outcomes. It is purely a perceptive judgment which forms an experience. It is you who will brand the experience as success or a failure, either ways, you are the master and you are right.

Obstacle Attractors

Despite the fact our action produces results and those results are perceived as an obstacle, failure or success, there seems to be a classification of individuals who have the tendency to attract more obstacles. And you know their fundamentals and drivers can be the basis for this classification, as all action flows from there.

You can call them as 'obstacle attractors' as they seem to have great affinity to consciously or unconsciously draw many obstacles towards them on their path to their goals.

You might have seen these individuals and worse still, you might be even one.

Please be on the lookout for these 'trait patterns', I mean individuals with the listed behavioral traits below who can fit the classification of 'obstacle attractors'.

Specific behavioral traits of OA's [Obstacle Attractors]

❖　　Day dreamers

❖　　Egotist

❖　　Pessimist

❖　　Perfectionist

❖　　Micro detailers

❖　　Negative orientors

❖　　Critics

❖　　Limiters

❖　　BHAG's

❖　　Dictators

❖　　Extreme emotions

❖　　Complex meddlers

❖　　Eternal beginner

❖　　Open minds

❖　　Unaccountable Actors

❖　　Attention Seekers

- ❖ Extreme Analysers

- ❖ Pushers

- ❖ Indecisive

- ❖ Plotters

- ❖ Timid

- ❖ Stallers

- ❖ Image mongers

- ❖ Rat Racers

- ❖ Complexity Meddlers

"My contemplation, should I or shouldn't I at times leads me to facing obstacles, I am working at overcoming it."

— Nadeemuddin, Corporate Fitness Coach & CEO,
Active Life Consulting

I wish you assess and check, if you possess some of the behavioral traits listed above, to understand how and why the obstacles and failures are drawn towards you.

If you do have some traits, my earnest suggestion for you is to shift from OA (obstacle attractors) to OM (obstacle managers) trait list at the earliest opportunity. It's possible, as all behavior is learned and though learning at adult stages is slow, nevertheless it is possible, if you have the will, enough need and a burning desire to change your behavior.

"I do feel through out my career 'decisiveness' helped me overcome obstacles whenever I have faced them."

- Narendra Luther, Former Chief Secretary & Author

Obstacle Managers

This classification of individuals have immense capability to encounter, experience and overcome any obstacle or failure at any phase of their life, provided they safeguard and upgrade regularly a very powerful set of behavioral traits they possess.

You would have met them, known about them, read about them or better still you might be even one of them. They are a very powerful bunch of people who have the necessary resources internally to 'Summit their Everest'.

A lot of conscious, conditioned and disciplined approach is needed to acquire, retain, upgrade and apply these effective traits which uniquely identify these individuals as 'Obstacle Managers'.

Specific behavioral traits of OM [Obstacle Managers]

❖ Initiators

❖ Optimists

❖ SMART goal managers

❖ Learners

❖ Child like

❖ Macro thinkers

❖ Open minds

❖ Effective memory

❖ Accountable Actors

❖ Adaptive

❖ Effective Role Model driven

❖ Decisive

❖ Planners

❖ Courageous

❖ Creative

❖ Delimiters

❖ Universal

❖ Effective planners

❖ Completers

❖ Big Thinkers

❖ Strategies

❖ Healthy Habits

❖ E.I enablers

❖ Non paranoids

❖ Socially Responsible

If you find yourself possessing some or all of these skill sets, go ahead and celebrate but do not forget to protect, as there are many obstacles and failures which can negatively impact you and overpower you in any times of adversity. But the above skill sets have the capacity to overcome most of the obstacles and failures. No wonder this classification is titled 'Obstacle Managers.' You better be one. : -)

"If we aren't willing to pay a price for our values, then we should ask ourselves whether we truly believe in those at all."

– Barack Obama, President, USA

IMPACT MODELS

5

IMPACT MODELS

FTA Model

This chapter is aimed at demystifying the amazing impact of obstacles, failures and success, on various dimensions of one's life, most importantly the 'fundamentals and the drivers' .

The below is a model which indicates how feelings, thoughts and actions get impacted by obstacles, failure and success.

Obstacle impact on FTA

"The ability to withstand the impact of obstacles & failures is what defines the real character of an individual. In good times nothing needs to be proven."

- Gen. K.V.Krishna Rao, Former Chief of Indian Army

As discussed earlier FTA (feelings, thoughts and actions) are fundamental units for all results in one's life and thereby they are the first to be impacted by results. As you are already aware by now, obstacles are none other than the perceptive outcomes of results.

There is no question that FTA gets impacted by obstacles. The severity of the impact naturally depends on the type and degree of the obstacles one encounters.

For example, a young executive considering his immediate boss an obstacle for his performance and growth, imagine the impact on his feelings, thoughts and actions, they can be stumbling blocks for his potential growth at work.

His feelings could be impacted by emotions like inconfidence and feelings of withdrawal, impacting which could be an array of disempowering, discouraging, limiting thoughts resulting in actions which are indecisive, unresourceful, unplanned and unaccountable.

"Once I hit a failure, all my actions will represent most of my feelings that I have experienced, they can be pretty turbulent"

– Venkatesh Mahadevan, Director IT, Asia, Motorola, India.

Time Factor

Repetitive obstacles within a shorter time frame can cause huge impact on FTA and could lead to deterioration of decision making capability, physical and mental vigor and also heavily reduce the speed of action. Time plays a crucial role in obstacles impacting FTA.

By spacing out goal units with a considerable gap, the obstacles could be well managed with an effective time put into it.

"I have learnt over the period of time, how I can overcome complex obstacles."

- Rajinikanth, News Presenter, TV9

Time in reference to the chronological age also impacts FTA differently. Certain type of obstacle with higher degree might not be well managed at an early age in one's life with less experience and lack of effective role models.

Even larger obstacles of various types and degrees can be managed well with more poise at later years of one's life, the age can come handy with plenty of past experiences and with effective role models. However, it's not necessary that it's true in all cases, as age necessarily need not accompany wisdom and can come all by itself.

What I mean to drive point here is that, time in reference to age of an individual will surely minimize or maximize the FTA, if the individual consciously designs his learning at all times.

Preparation

Being prepared for obstacles of any type and degree can cause less impact on FTA while being unprepared could cause more. Several obstacles can be well predicted, if one applies foresight as a skill to look beyond the obvious and plan for eventual and incidental obstacles.

It may not be possible to plan for all obstacles, but the one who foresees will be less impacted by obstacles on FTA.

The clarity of goals, focus on action to reach those goals, skills and habits of planning can help individual fabulously reduce the impact of obstacles on FTA.

Positive Angle

The impact of obstacles on FTA is at times positive and can encourage you. It could prepare the individual for effective future management of obstacles, so not all impact on FTA by obstacles is negative. Some of the memories of past feelings while experiencing obstacles can be great lessons for avoiding future mishaps.

Failure & Success Impact

The impact of failure and success on FTA could be as extreme as the interpretation of the results. Failure impacts FTA very deeply and has an influence of longevity of the impact experience. Large failure has large impacts.

Failure Impact

For those who are weak and get negatively impacted by even small failures, the impact of large failure could be almost fatal. One's capability to cope with the failures of all shapes and sizes can help to reduce the tremendous impact of failure on FTA.

Letting failure impact FTA especially in larger failures and not attempting to reduce and divert the impact could lead to extreme feelings like depression, suicidal thoughts, and actions which could possibly lead to fatal consequences.

It's important for individuals to not let failure impact FTA to an extreme. Lack of confidence, lack of self respect, disloyalty, lack of focus, loss of credibility, missed precision and low motivation can be some of the outcomes of failure impact on FTA.

Success Impact

'Success breeds success' has been in circulation from the time unknown and I believe it's true in a sense that, success impacts FTA in a very effective way, encouraging and reinforcing 'empowering beliefs'. It revitalizes values and increases the speed of action by strengthening the power of decision making and planning, eventually leading to more success.

There are cases where individuals not drawing inspiration from their past success have been exposed to potential failure, immediately after success. Registering the experience of Success and impacting the FTA is crucial for 'success to breed more success.'

I strongly recommend learning more proactively from 'success' than failures. Failures automatically put you in a mode of learning, and most of the time the learning is compulsive to survive, in the times of adversity.

But while basking in the glory of success, learning can be bare minimum, unless there is a proactive attempt to draw lessons in the midst of all the celebration that success drives. It's very important that one learns from success too.

There are historic examples of success breeding failure with larger than life iconic superstars of sports, business, music and movies who are reduced to dismal failures, in just few years of their rise to glory.

You can figure out, if you study their lives that most of them were too busy to learn right lessons while their success lasted and the impact of their success on their FTA was not empowering enough, to let them stay on the top.

Managing success is as important as managing failure if one doesn't want 'failure to succeed... success '.

Cause & Effect Model

A farmer started a crop season in his fields by sowing paddy. Over the season he did what any farmer would do; perform a set of actions to eventually reap the yield at the end of the season.

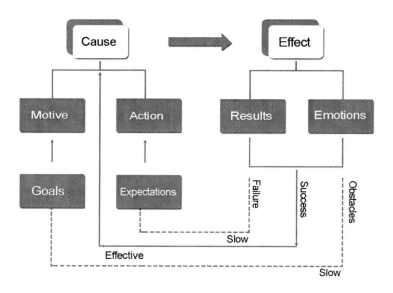

What will the yield be ? You might be amused at this question. Of course paddy, the rice. Now tell me, would it be right for the farmer to expect cotton as the yield instead of paddy? Is it naturally possible for the yield to change?

The above reference might seem a little unscientific; but actually it's very scientific, natural and very powerful. Imagine how many times you have wanted different results, with the same set of actions performed by you.

❖   I will be who I am – I want everyone to respect me.

❖   I want great results – I will do what I always do.

❖   I want to have lasting relationships – I will do what I always do.

❖   I want to grow to the next level at work – I can't possibly do more, than what I am already doing.

❖   I want to be famous and popular – I don't want to work for it.

❖   I want great wealth – I don't know how to go about it.

❖   I want to be a great father – I am already doing my best.

❖   I want to shed 5 kgs of excess fat – I cannot work out.

There are many such paradoxes we go through in our life every day, without realizing the fact that there is a system working along with us, as we act.

Welcome to 'Cause & Effect'[C & E], the model is very scientific and makes you responsible for everything you feel, think and do. If you get what you deserve from your actions, you should not complain, whether it is positive or negative. In fact it's you, who at the first place, made it happen.

Cause and effect is about a set of actions leading to an outcome. There is an amount of certainty in this cycle and very less surprises. If I deploy certain actions, they are bound to result in certain outcomes. In the farmer's case, sowing paddy is a set of actions bundled with many others to grow the crop and the effect is the yield, which is paddy.

Cause and effect is as simple. 'What you sow is what you reap'.

Every cycle of cause and effect has a potential to be an obstacle, failure or success. The impact of obstacle on this cycle is direct, intense and at times extreme.

Individuals quitting their set goals by facing obstacles or failures are mostly the victims of the impact on cause and effect cycle.

I am of the belief that, if one even accepts the Cause & Effect cycle, their preparedness towards obstacles and failures will be far superior to those who have no knowledge of it. In fact, you will hardly have anyone to blame for your obstacles and failures, but you.

I strongly feel, educating children with this model helps the child to learn responsible action based on consequence analysis. All that 'school shootouts' reported in USA and India is the result of non-consequential action by these children, who are hardly ever taught to be accountable for their actions and understand the consequences.

There are nations, who unleash certain set of actions either through their international policies with other nations at times exhibiting utter lack of understanding of the consequences of their actions. Their lack of understanding in 'cause and effect' can lead them to take decisions for temporary reprieve, which can result in disastrous implications.

Cause & Effect is even applicable to a larger framework like a nation and its policies and outcomes as much as it is to an individual action and outcomes. Organizational, institutional and social applications of C&E yield same results.

"I know that if I don't move towards my goals, my goals do not move towards me."

- Rahul Dev, Movie Actor

Responsibility of leadership, delegation and effective communication, mutual respect, motivations are few of the skills which result out of the knowledge of cause & effect.

For example a good leader will know that a set of actions in the form of communication can result either in demotivation or motivation (cause and effect); his cautious approach towards the action, is what eventually is recognized as an effective leadership.

On the other hand, one who is not cautious or wary of his actions and results (C&E) can be recognized more for his callousness and unaccountability than for leadership. Most of the 'vision' for individuals, family, organization and nations are designed by those, who believe in cause and effect.

Failure & Success Impact

Failure and success impact C&E. The outcomes of the impact are also very similar to that of FTA.

The impact of success on cause and effect can lead to confidence, cautiousness or extreme risk appetite as impact outcomes. As consequential and accountable action most often than not, yields great results. Especially, if assessed in the long run.

123

Likewise, failure impact on C&E could be on an extreme end as dramatic as leading you to shy away from all proactive action, fearing a repulsive outcome and be reduced to floating blocks of wood in the flow of events in one's life.

There are even instances, where individuals stop initiating action and be on the receiving end of what situations lead them into, as they lose all power and strength to act after consistent and dismal failures. The consistent failure of their actions, prohibit them from acting, as they are almost in the fear of the consequences.

Learning from the impact of obstacle, failure and success on cause & effect can influence one's attitude towards life, goal setting, plan of action and results.

Belief Impact Model

Beliefs have been deeply defined, analyzed and understood in the earlier chapters and by now you must be aware of their sensitivity to the environment and situations.

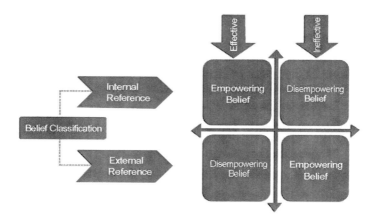

Beliefs have astounding impact on obstacles and while under impact from the same. Small, medium, large obstacles of any type can impact and shake the foundation (reference system) and reference legs of the beliefs.

Beliefs which are externally referential are most impacted by obstacles and transform. There are times when large obstacles can impact beliefs so much that the entire belief disappears.

For example, the untimely death of a loved one in the family can impact your beliefs on 'God', so much that you stop believing god. Loosing beliefs on one's religion as a result of certain obstacles is one of the major reasons for people converting their religions.

A belief as big as 'one's religion', can change with the impact of obstacles.

A near death experience in a helicopter accident, several years back for Dr. Abdul Kalam, his Excellency former President of India, has resulted in drastic change in few of his beliefs. He even quoted this incident in his book 'Wings of Fire'.

A life threatening obstacle of that size impacted his beliefs so much that certain beliefs disappeared and certain new were formed. In his personal interaction with me, he shared how his new set of very positive beliefs invigorated his life, since then.

It is not necessary that all change is for good or all change is for bad outcomes. Objectively, one has to be in a position to assess the changes after an obstacle impact to analyze the effective and ineffective impacts on 'Beliefs'.

Longevity – Memory Impact

Impact of obstacle on belief is linked mostly to the memory of an individual. Those who have lasting memory of all characteristics of an obstacle they encounter, they will also remember the process, events and skills or the lack of it, which lead to an obstacle and also remember the process of overcoming or surrendering to an obstacle.

"In the toughest times of my life, I survived with my family and fans by my side."

— Ms. Aarti Agarwal, Movie Actress

These individual's beliefs are impacted very deeply and for a very long time while those with less memory access could have lower impact on their beliefs comparatively for a less duration of time.

There's a possibility that you fall into the trap of immensely limiting beliefs and experience helplessness and incapability to set larger goals.

The popular adage 'rich become richer, poor poorer' comes from a similar reference.

The possibility of the poor people working on this adage, keeps them poor for all their lives, as they seem to believe the phrase very strongly, that it disempowers any effort to break the norm and act towards, 'poor can become rich'.

On the other hand the adage is advantageous for those who internalize the adage that 'Rich become richer' and it automatically can drive the power of action towards a certain outcome, richer outputs.

Support System

Support systems can make a huge difference when prolonged experience of obstacles negatively impact beliefs. Friends, family, social group support can avert extreme impact on beliefs by obstacles.

'Obstacles can make a cat out of a tiger or tiger out of a cat'. The belief of one's capability can either be challenged by an obstacle, which can accentuate skills to surmount it or can overwhelm so that you quit under the influence.

'If you challenge the obstacles, they wouldn't incapacitate you'. Protecting your empowering beliefs and internalizing is the key for effective obstacle management to reduce the negative impact of obstacles on your beliefs.

Value Impact Model

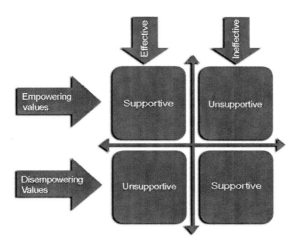

As explained earlier, a set of priorities which drive all thoughts and actions are 'values'.

The impact of obstacles on values is crucial and path breaking, literally. Most of the goal units are driven by prioritized values and when they encounter an obstacle, either the values drive action to overcome or recede to give in.

Obstacles have the capability to re-organize, rearrange, or erase your values. Your conviction on your value list and value sequence is the key criteria for assessing impact.

For example, Mahatma Gandhi's top value 'freedom' has never 'given in' to any impact despite decades of consistent, repetitive obstacle and failure experiences.

His primary value strongly supported by internalized empowering belief such as 'non violence' had helped Gandhi withstand the pressure from external environment. I don't think anyone can question his conviction to that value called 'Freedom'.

Conviction to values, capabilities to build supporting beliefs can be a successful process to reduce the negative impact of obstacles on values.

In everyday life, minor obstacle might not impact values as much as large obstacles will, eventually. Being on guard to analyze the impact of obstacles on values can help one safeguard one's empowering values.

If your values are vulnerable to the impact of the external obstacles, it is certain that your values are bound to shift periodically resulting in loss of credibility and consistency of goals.

For example, if minor obstacles can influence individuals to change goals regularly, 'quitting does become a habit'. There are hardly any successful individuals who have this habit.

Pay attention to your micro and grand goals. These are actual reflections of your values. If your value system is 'empowering' then regular change of macro and grand goals is a far possibility. However, any changes can reflect your internal value conflict.

Change of goals for better opportunities is different than change of goals to escape obstacle, those of us who regularly change our goals to escape obstacles or to take a detour from them are only demonstrating the lack of stable 'empowered value system'.

Obstacles and failures can also drive new values in one's life. At times drastic failures or insurmountable obstacles can create a new set of empowering values and may result in an individual driving himself in a very different direction than usual to succeed.

For example, the incapacitating accident was a huge personal obstacle where in Christopher Reeves almost turned from a superman to a mere vegetable. The obstacle did impact his values hard by creating a new set of values which has driven Mr. Reeves to again attain greater heights, this time fighting a worthy cause for 'Stem Cell Research'.

Whether it is Mahatma Gandhi, Martin Luther King Junior, Helen Keller, Mother Teresa, Arnold Schwarzenegger, or even Barack Obama, they all have been impacted by crucial obstacles before transforming themselves into someone else, who is driven to attain global goals.

Everyone of those and many who have attained greater success have acquired new set of values which drove them towards that destination on the advent of an obstacle.

"There is no area in life, which is not negatively affected by obstacles and failures, as long as you let it."

- Prem Chand Degra, Mr. Universe,
Professional Body Builder

OBSTACLE OUTCOMES

OBSTACLE OUTCOMES

6

Obstacles & failures have very impressive outcomes. Some are compellingly progressive and add value to individuals by enhancing their 'power to cope', 'learning experience for future', 'forming new empowering beliefs', 'forming effective references', 'challenging resources' , 'driving passion' and ' driving action', while others could be compellingly regressive and impact individuals through 'ineffective beliefs', 'discouraging references', 'lowering standards', 'facilitating compromise' , 'quitting goals' , 'giving up aspirations', 'driving depression'.

Let's look at how several critical facets of your personality are impacted by obstacles. The knowledge of this impact can increase your consciousness towards focusing on these areas in the times of adversity to check the impact and make corrections to effectively overcome.

31

Obstacles & Emotions

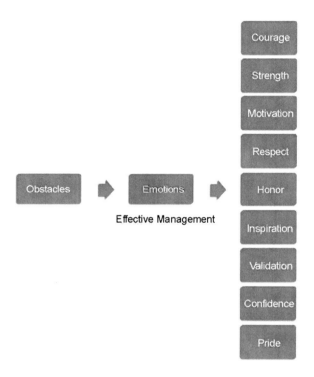

The obstacle impact is also discussed in the FTA model very clearly. Here I will highlight the outcomes. There are several emotions which are triggered internally when you encounter an obstacle.

Large obstacles either perceived or in real drive higher degree emotions while smaller obstacles tend to trigger lower degree emotions.

"I do feel saddened when I find myself helpless to correct the corrupt system."

- Vijaya Rama Rao, Former CBI Director & Minister for State

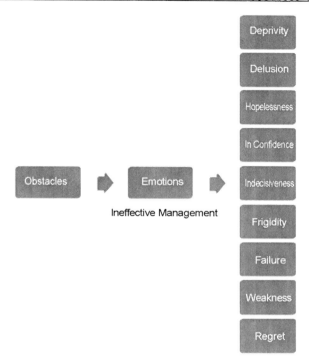

It is important that you understand and measure your affinity to get affected by obstacles and especially so, while encountering the larger ones. Emotions can play havoc with one's capability to manage obstacles.

As one of the key fundamentals, any affect on this component will impact the entire framework of obstacle management effectively or ineffectively.

In conflict, emotion is the driver of an obstacle, the impact of the same will be felt heavily as a result. In the entire process of how someone identifies an obstacle to how they end up managing depends solely on ones 'emotional intelligence'.

As emotions are spontaneous responses to any sensory perception, they are bound to be reactive unless there is a conscious attempt to delay the response to avoid reactive tendencies. The amount of time one takes to cope with a higher degree obstacle or failure is one of the core parameters which showcases their emotional intelligence capability.

The Possible Outcome

❖ Emotions of disbelief and deprivity.

❖ Emotions of frigidity and feelings of hopelessness.

❖ Emotions of weakness and lack of direction, feelings of loosing track, feelings of regret, feelings of wronged action and feelings of indecisiveness are possibilities.

❖ Emotions of strength, feelings of direction, feelings of certainty, motivation, inspiration and feelings of validation and courage, while overcoming obstacles

❖ Emotions of vindication, pride, confidence, triumph, feelings of resourcefulness, respect, honour and feeling of success after overcoming obstacles and failures.

How to manage

❖ Enabling you consciously with emotional intelligence (EI) helps manage the impact.

❖ Practicing delayed gratification to resist reactive tendencies.

❖ Using visualization as a tool to minimize perceptive impact.

❖ By having SMART and large grand goals.

❖ Being conscious of all those emotions which are driving you away from your goals while you face obstacles.

❖ Fostering and nurturing effective emotions which can help you overcome obstacles and failures.

❖ Shielding your effective emotions consciously to protect them from the negative impact.

Consciously monitoring the impact of obstacles and failures on your emotions can shield emotions from being ineffectively impacted by adversity. Emotional intelligence plays a crucial role in protecting and salvaging one's emotions in the rough path of reaching grand goals interspersed by many obstacles and failures.

Obstacles & Decision Making

"It's likely to slow the decision making. In the case of a failure the individual may question his or her ability to make good decisions in the future hence he or she becomes "stuck" in an indecisive mode. In the case of obstacles, if the individual feels overwhelmed then I believe a common reaction is to do nothing."

- Prof. Kathleen A Krentler, Professor of Marketing,
San Diego State University, SDSU

Obstacles have lasting impact on decision making. Most of the obstacles are decisions which did not reach their predetermined objective. As every action unit is a decision, every time an action results in unattained objective, the past decision to act is in question.

135

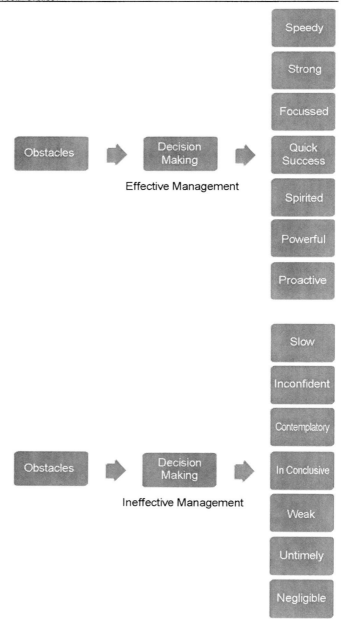

There are very few individuals who have the capability to continue with effective decision making despite high degree obstacles and failures. Their capability to face cynicism both externally and internally in reference to their decisions is stronger than those individuals, whose decisions when questioned tend to either weaken, delay or stalled.

If you are driving your decisions without the support of your empowering goals and beliefs, if your decisions are based on passion than on logic, if your decisions are not resulting in accountable action, they are bound to get negatively impacted by the obstacles.

If your decision making process is supported by empowering values, beliefs and attitude directed towards your SMART goals with focus and a strong reference management, the decisions will be less impacted negatively.

"My role in different positions in the army taught me many tough lessons. Especially to make effective decisions, even while I am under extreme pressure."

- Major General Mahanjan,
Former Commandant, College of Defence Management

There is a noticeable shift onto a slow decision making process, when one encounters obstacles or failures consistently. At times the impact could be so high that there are hardly any decisions which are made in that phase.

The fear of making wrong decisions can freeze the entire decision making process.

There are certain phases where for weeks and months decisions are not made and action either completely stalls or becomes negligible.

Imagine a phase of consistent failure and follow the decision making pattern in that phase to get an idea of the impact of failure on decision making.

The possible outcomes

❖ Obstacles impact decision both directly and indirectly.

❖ Obstacles not effectively managed will have adverse affect on decision making.

❖ Obstacles left to pile up or neglected without resolution can weaken the decision making process.

❖ Large obstacles which seem to be insurmountable after periodic attempts to overcome can pose question to the quality of decision making.

❖ Unmanaged obstacles can lead to decisions made with less choices and can be weak and ineffective.

❖ Decisions made in the midst of failing obstacle management can yet times lead you away from your goals.

❖ Extremely emotional decisions are possible in the times of adversity and can sometimes even be fatal.

❖ Balanced decision making with emotion and logic seems challenging in times of adversity.

❖ Large obstacle and consistent failures can shake the foundation of decision making process.

How to manage

"My decision to add value to others through social service very early in my life sometimes does get attacked as a selfish motive once a while by the distractors, but as my goals are clear & values are in order, I evaluate the impact of these small obstacles and move on with more resolve to do good to the world I live in."

- Dr. Ravi Vadlamani,
Past District Governor 3150, Rotary International

❖   Being aware of the decisions which are driving obstacles.

❖   Being prepared to deal with obstacles and their impact on decisions.

❖   Knowing your decision making process and developing the capability to assess the impact.

❖   Making proactive choices for effective decision making.

❖   Refrain from reactive and exaggerated emotional decisions.

❖   Attempt to be in control of the decisions you are making for yourself and others.

❖   Apply both passion and rationale in making decisions which impact your goals.

Obstacles & Confidence

"If someone says he can, I believe he can"

– Prof.Adrian Kennedy, Managing Director, Apollo Wellness RX

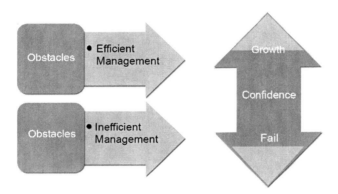

Confidence is the outcome of the quantification of all the positive results either in real or so perceived by you. It's not easy to experience a massive negative result out of your action and still feel confident about it in future. Confidence does get impacted by obstacles and failures.

Beliefs impact confidence and results impact beliefs. Impacted beliefs can either strengthen to become more powerful or weaken to lose its reference framework.

In the attempt to reach your goals, all the action units you deploy are bound to give results and they can in turn impact beliefs. The impact on belief is directly expressed in the confidence to act further.

Smaller obstacles have considerably lower impact in comparison to that of larger one's which tend to yet times shift the entire belief base thereby impacting the confidence at its roots.

Some examples

A political candidate who lost his elections three times consecutively will have by then lost confidence in his constituents to vote him to power in the next election.

A doctor, whose heart operations failed consistently thrice costing patient's lives in a week, will of course lead to some inconfidence at the surgery table the very next time.

I can't take the name of a student from the school where I am currently completing my Ph.D work, whose confidence rock bottomed in the last one year of his passing out from MBA program as a very intelligent, smart and vocal student who has great career opportunities awaiting.

He has been from job to job over 3 times in the last year alone and at every shift and at every next interview, he is losing some confidence from his overall system. Recently I met him, and was surprised to see a completely shattered, confused, lost and in confident man.

Empathizing with him, and understanding him completely after an hour spent with him, I did express that most of his obstacles are perceived and not real, and few of those which are real were also not that big to fight. I figured he has issues with his value list and sequence and now I am in the process of helping him out of the situation, he is in. Perceived or Real obstacles can play havoc with your confidence.

As reported in several media channels, the sacking of Mr.Charu Sharma, the CEO of the Royal Challenge IPL team, is the result of loss of confidence on his leadership capabilities as perceived by Dr.Vijay Mallya.

141

Dr.Mallya's decision for sure is not based out of one defeat; there should be more to it. Is it judicious? Who am I or the media to ask? The impact on confidence is as personal as it can get, and an individual has a right to act on that basis.

Large obstacles which seem to be insurmountable do have a huge impact on confidence either temporarily or yet times permanently depending on the reference system and belief structure of an individual.

There are few exceptional cases where in adversity and large obstacles have incremented one's confidence to set larger goals or to keep moving the existing goals with more fervor. The ability of certain individuals to protect their confidence and be challenged to increase their attempts to succeed while they face adversity is the key for this exception.

It is a fact that extraordinary heroes of our time and in the past haven't attained their glory by 'not failing', but by their will and capability to get up after 'every fall and be stronger than before'. The sheer confidence in their actions despite repeat failures seems to be the key to all success they have attained against all odds.

The possible outcome

❖   An obstacle does impact confidence.

❖   Confidence is the outcome of consistent positive results either perceived or in real.

❖   The result assessment in real or in perception can lead to the impact on confidence.

❖   Repeat failures can impact confidence either temporarily or permanently.

❖ Specific 'confidence areas' can get affected by 'specific results'.

❖ At times the impact of obstacles and failures is not specific to a certain 'confidence area' and can impact overall confidence.

❖ There is a possibility of a positive impact of obstacles on confidence at times, when adversity drives more action and decisiveness.

❖ Extra ordinary ability to protect confidence from being negatively impacted, can lead to, successfully overcoming large obstacles and failures.

❖ Obstacle impact on confidence can be a very good measure to determine one's capability to overcome obstacles.

How to manage

❖ By being aware of your empowering and disempowering beliefs.

❖ By internalizing your effective beliefs regularly.

❖ Judging the sources of your confidence and managing them effectively.

❖ Building resources through strong references to support your confidence in the times of adversity.

❖ By choosing effective role models.

❖ By choosing effective mentors & coaches.

❖ By attempting to succeed smaller goals for strengthening and gaining confidence on a regular basis.

❖ To protect your confidence from assault of obstacle and failures consciously.

Obstacles & Goals

"I will neither sleep, nor let you sleep while I pursue goals to make this state 'Swarna Andhrapradesh'."

- Chandra Babu Naidu, Former Chief Minister,
Andhra Pradesh

It is 'goals' which are the most affected of all while encountering, experiencing and overcoming an obstacle.

Obstacles and failures impact your goals than anything else can. All the talk of you redefining goals, regrouping resources, reassessing capabilities and even abandoning your goals apply, only while obstacles and failures impact them.

Short, medium and long term goals get impacted differently by different types and degree of obstacles. Large obstacles can impact even your long term grand goals while the smaller one's can impact your micro and smaller goal units.

Visualize individuals quitting their goals. Most often than not, it is out of direct impact of obstacles and failures. Goals are primarily achieved by overcoming the obstacles in the way. When ineffective management of obstacles occur, the delay in achieving one's goals can impact the current goal units and even the grand goal.

As understood in the SOF Model in the first chapter, every action unit leads to results and the perception of results can lead to obstacles and failures subsequently. If your goal setting process (GSP) drives

SMART goals, there is a good possibility of managing obstacles on the way and reduce the impact directly on goals.

"In my career as army chief or as a governor, I always did what is expected of me, to reach my goals. I made a choice, to not let anything stop me. Nothing could ever stop me from reaching the goals I had set, not even the attempts to eliminate me."

– Gen.K.V.Krishna Rao, Former Chief of Indian Army & Former Governor for Jammu & Kashmir

If your goals are unscientifically set BHAG's [Big Hairy Audacious Goals] the impact of obstacles is directly felt several times over in comparison to that of SMART goals. The GSP plays a crucial role in either accentuating or reducing the impact of obstacles on the goals.

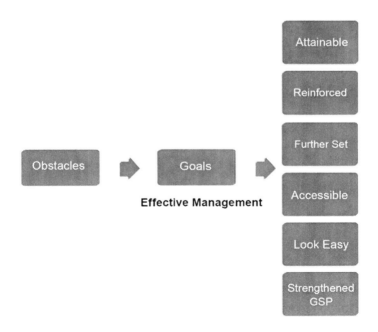

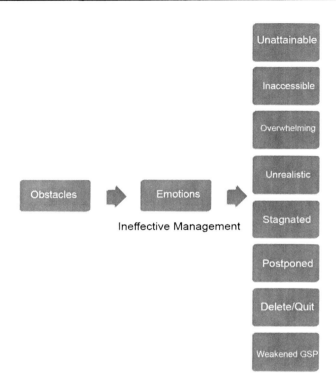

Lack of grand goals can make smaller goal units (micro goals) vulnerable to the negative impact, while having one can make a lot of difference.

Individuals with focused SMART goals paired with grand goals will have 'higher coping capability' in comparison to those who lack them.

For example, my vision of being one of the largest service provider in telecom in the entire world, can give me ample strength to overlook and override many obstacles which are bound to be in my way, while I pursue a grand goal of that size.

While the grandeur of the final goal can keep the hope 'on', even the largest obstacles in the process can be surmounted with the spirit of achieving that great goal.

Mostly either you allow goals to be impacted or you don't. The power of choice which we will discuss in later chapters is the key attribute to resist the impact of obstacles on goals.

It is imperative, that your choice to protect your goals is driven out of your commitment to existing goal units and passion to attain the larger grand goal. In the process of attaining multiple goals, individuals lacking passion and logic can have a difficult time.

Consistently finding effective solutions to nagging obstacles and failures by self motivated and focused individuals, can shield the impact considerably.

Protecting one's goal from getting negatively impacted is representative of one's capability to manage obstacles and failures.

The possible impacts

❖ Goals do get impacted by obstacles and failures. In fact they are the most affected.

❖ Short, medium and long term goals get impacted differently by different sizes and degrees of obstacles.

❖ Having grand goals can be helpful to shield considerable impact of even large obstacles and failures.

❖ Lack of grand goals can accentuate the negative impact of obstacles on all sets of goals.

❖ Power of your 'choice' to allow goals to be impacted or protected is driven out of both passion and rational in managing obstacles in attaining grand goals.

❖ Regular review of your goals to assess the validity of GSP can help reduce negative impact.

❖ Goal management strategies at every mile stone can help one prepare to encounter, experience and manage the obstacles on the way.

❖ Most situations of abandoning goals are raised out of mismanagement and untimely resolution of obstacles.

How to manage

❖ To have a scientific goal setting process (GSP).

❖ To have SMART and large grand goals.

❖ To have persistence and courage to pursue.

❖ By consistent and regular review of the obstacle impact.

❖ By using 'methods to summit' in the later chapters to overcome.

❖ By achieving smaller goals and celebrating for stronger reference.

❖ By consciously protecting goals from the impact of obstacles and failures.

❖ Through professional planning and preparation for goal management.

Obstacles & Focus

"I am aware that there will be thousand obstacles for the projects, I have undertaken in my tenure as chief minister for this state, but nothing can affect my focus. We will overcome all the obstacles & surely reach the goals."

- Dr. Y.S. Rajashekar Reddy, Chief Minister, Andhra Pradesh

'Focus' and its importance to attain goals cannot be stressed more; you surely need to attain deeper understanding of this 'driver'.

Focus can drive you towards obstacles or towards your goals. It boils down to where your focus is, goals or obstacles. The impact of obstacles on focus is critical and has immense impact on the overall obstacle and failure management process.

Obstacles can impact your focus by diversion, delusion and depravity. There are many instances where obstacles can hinder individual's capability to stay focused on the task at hand and divert to other areas which are of minimal importance and relevance to reach one's goals.

There is a history of catastrophic results through 'lack of focus' and when you get to the root of it, you will easily figure out certain obstacles would have shifted the focus.

The focus on one's large goals is one of the prime reasons why individuals learn, plan, sustain and act despite all odds. Obstacles have a critical characteristic of impacting this focus at every stage of encounter. If you look at the definition of the obstacle in earlier chapters it is evident that there is a slow down while one encounters an obstacle, it could be temporary or permanent depending on one's capability and resolve to manage and to reach larger goals.

"I bet you can never lose an inch of your fat, if you don't have focus. All those who shape up with my personal training are those, who keep their excuses aside and focus on the goal to 'shut up & shape up'."

– Nadeemuddin, Fitness Coach,
Consultant & CEO of Active Life Consulting

Focus is a key contributor to success in all its forms and no wonder, it is one of the most important drivers which gets impacted on the advent of an obstacle or a failure.

I know of individuals whose focus is drifted mostly towards obstacles as they seem to have a head full of possibilities of obstacles, while they tread towards their goals and in their attempt to be prepared for all those probable obstacles, most of their resources are focused towards these perceived obstacles than goals.

The possible outcome

❖ Focus is one of the early drivers to get impacted.

❖ Obstacles trigger diversion of focus as a primary symptom of an encounter.

❖ The impact on focus can affect the whole process of obstacle and failure management.

❖ The impact of focus can lead to a slow down, deter, quitting or even driving in the opposite direction of a set goal.

❖ It is one of the most powerful factors to get impacted at the early stages of the encounter.

How to manage

❖ To have a scientific goal setting process (GSP).

❖ To have SMART and large grand goals.

❖ By being conscious of assessing one's focus periodically.

❖ By not getting over indulgent and over conscious in the process of planning for effective obstacle management , so that your focus is more on obstacles than on goals.

❖ By being disciplined in the process of both goal setting and goal management.

Obstacles & Relationships

Almost all relationships are susceptible to the impact of obstacles. I believe it's neither natural nor ideal for obstacles and failures to impact relationships and yet most of the times they do.

Social conditioning and individual incapability to keep relationships at a safe distance from obstacles and failures seems to be the reason why it happens.

There are times, relationships could themselves be obstacles.

As you face large obstacles or failures, there is a great possibility of your immediate relationships getting negatively impacted for various reasons. One of the primary reasons being their lost confidence in your decisions and actions. Sometimes these presumptive conclusions of your incapability, even while you are in the process of managing adversity can add more fuel to the fire.

Matured relationships do not need to feel unsettled or be impacted negatively by obstacle and failure. The competence of individuals in your relationships to be emotionally intelligent and focused on your common goals is the key. If they focus on your obstacles, it can lead to several ineffective feelings which can drive instability in relationships.

I strongly believe, it is emotion which drives all impact on relationships during one's adversity. Personal relationships are the easiest to get affected in the times of failure, social and professional relationships will not be left too far behind especially when individuals in those relationships are not emotionally intelligent.

There are several instances where individuals have lost all relationships inclusive of their closest relationships like mother & father, Spouse & children disowning or abandoning them, while they struggle to overcome large obstacles and at times miserable failures.

This also showcases the obstacle manager's incapability to sustain relationships by investing resources especially in adverse times.

The possible outcome

❖   There is a considerable and visual impact on relationship of all forms by obstacles and failures.

❖   The impact can strain, unsettle and yet times can destroy relationships.

❖   Professional relationships are the easiest to get impacted at adversity; personal and social will follow suit, if not well managed.

❖ The impact on relationships can be so harsh that new obstacles can crop up while you are struggling to manage the earlier.

❖ Lack of trust and emotional intelligence are critical to the impact.

❖ The obstacle managers 'relationship management' skills are crucial for your success at managing effective relationship in adversity.

How to manage

❖ 'Relationship management' needs to be consistently practiced and not just in adversity.

❖ 'Give and take' in a relationship needs to be balanced and consistent, to manage effective relationships.

❖ Trust needs to be fostered and nurtured at all times to effectively manage.

❖ Separating relationship equation from 'action results' can lead to a long term harmony. Separating personal, professional, social and global relationships and their goals can help.

❖ Maturity, empathy, strength, courage and focus are the keys to manage the impact of obstacles.

❖ Your ability to be not unnerved and stand tall during testing times by protecting and supporting your empowering values and beliefs can drive effectiveness thereby reduce the impact.

❖ Non reactionary response and expression of frustrations and anxiety in relationships across board, while in the process of encountering, experiencing and managing large obstacles and failures can immensely help.

Obstacles & Physiology

Despite the fact that physiology and its response to obstacles and failures vary tremendously across the world based on several demographic, geographic and anthropological factors, there are certain standard possibilities which tend to express themselves in times of adversity.

The emotional impact of obstacles is transferred to the physiology through the channel of 'attitude' (state of mind). An unresourceful state of mind can transform your physiology to be more vulnerable to the external impact.

The impact on physiology is expressed in many forms starting with tiresomeness, plain weakness, a headache and hypertension to severe abnormalities such as cardiac issues, respiratory and nervous issues. A full blown impact of obstacles or a failure is felt through the sensory organs which perceive it and transfer the load to the entire system.

There are several instances of individuals losing physical strength, stamina and even sexual vitality while in the process of managing large obstacles and failures. Factors such as blood pressure, indigestion, insomnia, loss of appetite, reckless eating (bingeing), slowing metabolic activity, less acute sensory organs, loss of resistance to disease are some of the very evident signs of obstacle impact on physiology.

On the extreme, a study on 'workplace ills' reported that, employees in the grip of stress can even forget to breathe actively and completely, which eventually paves way for serious respiratory and cardiac issues.

154

I personally feel individuals with less disciplined system of managing physiology, have good probability of being on the 'receiving end' while attempting to manage obstacles and failures.

In contrary, those who train their bodies to be fit, active and nourish with right nutrition are endowed with immense capability to withstand the impact of obstacles and failures. The coping mechanism is strong in healthy bodies, while it is vulnerable and weak in unhealthy bodies.

The possible outcome

❖ Obstacles and failures do impact the physiology.

❖ The amount of impact and resistance is dependent on how well the bodies are trained to cope.

❖ Unprepared and malnourished physiology is a 'sitting duck' for stress related impacts of obstacles and failures.

❖ Frivolous health hassles to large physiological system failures and at times leading to fatal consequences is the impact outcome.

❖ Different people react and express the obstacle impact differently; some tend to exhibit the signs of impact immediately after an encounter while others take ample time to exhibit.

How to manage

❖ By preparing your body, to not adversely respond to mental stress easily.

❖ By disassociating mind and body and allowing the mental fatigue and fear to find ways of expression, than through the harmful physical expression.

❖ By regular physical exercises and active lifestyle.

❖ By nourishing the body with high quality nutrients and taking good care of health and hygiene.

❖ By training your body to withstand stress and related obstacle impacts.

❖ By having regular medical checkups and getting professional help, when in need.

Obstacles & Finances

"Most of the failures, I have seen are from miserable financial planning & unrealistic financial goals."

- Ravi Barla, Senior Branch Head, JM Financial

One of the hardest hit in the process of obstacle and failure management, especially in the middle and lower income group, could be finances.

Your finances could themselves be obstacles. Either the result of an obstacle mismanaged, or a failure, can lead to a financial impact.

Despite how rich and wealthy one may get, the desire to acquire more can lead to potential obstacles at the top end of the pyramid, where the wealthy few stay. While the majority at the bottom might have obstacles driven out of lack of financial capabilities to fulfill their basic needs.

In a society where the home you own, the car you drive and the class you belong to, take precedence over any other measure of success, there's bound to be obstacles at every step of the way, in a constant attempt to scale up one's socio economic status.

'I am concerned about how rich you are, and not how you are that rich', the bleak ethical and moral situation in the course of acquiring wealth, and majority's validation of any means to make money, can in the long run cause bitter battles internally and externally leading to either large obstacles or failures.

Inspired by ineffective role models and a fast forward, lavish lifestyle, individuals taking short cuts to succeed in terms of wealth acquisition can lead to disastrous results, if the consequential obstacle & failures in the way are not managed effectively.

Obstacles and failures can lead to diversion of resources and can impact one's financial resources during adversity. Having a well designed and customized personal financial plan, setting smart financial goals both micro and grand as early in one's life can help avert the negative impact.

The possible impacts

❖	Obstacles have the propensity to impact finances at almost all socio economic levels in their own magnitude.

❖	Either the outcome of mismanaged obstacles can lead to financial issues and failures or an obstacle from a different classification can impact finances indirectly.

❖	Lack of planning, smart goals and financial indiscipline can drive many obstacles.

157

How to manage

❖   By having smart micro and macro financial goals.

❖   By practicing strict financial discipline and being in control of your financial situation.

❖   By increasing your capability to foresee potential obstacles and failures in your financial domain.

❖   By being cautious and acting on obstacles and failures on time to avoid a pile up which can lead to disastrous impact on your finances.

❖   By analyzing every obstacle's possible impact on your finances and being prepared to manage the same.

Obstacles & Environment

"While I am frustrated and encountering obstacles, I do get moody and can affect people around me, in the immediate environment".

– Anuradha Venkatesh, Executive HR, Satyam

Obstacles do have a measurable impact on the environment which is defined by relationships, family, work place, neighborhood, society and geographical region.

There are no ripples, if there is no action. It's like a stone thrown in a pond. The magnitude of the impact on the environment depends on the size and degree of an obstacle or a failure. The impact is also varying in different cultural and social scenarios depending on multiple factors which influence individual's environment.

"Half the battle is won, if you have the confidence on your decisions & the path you have chosen as the final one."

– Dr. Jayaprakash Narayan, Founder President, Loksatta Party

For example, the impact of a failure of an individual by the environment could be very high in certain socio geographic areas in India, with extreme intrusion of extended family and society into individual lives to make judgements. And the same might not be the case for an individual failing in USA, but they might have several other issues which impact the environment, which are unique to their society.

There are times while the magnitude of one's failure could be small, but the impact of it in the environment and the resultant response from the environment can magnify a failure several times over to negatively impact one's confidence and resources, thereby limiting their ability to overcome.

It is evident that the impact of obstacles and failures on 'environment' is much smaller in comparison to the environment's impact on obstacles and failures. At times the magnitude of the impact is so huge that individuals give up their life in the fear of not just failure, but the possible persecution by the society and the environment at large.

In reference to India, there are several examples of young students, choosing death after their failure in their examinations. Couples in love ending their lives in fear of social obstacles. Farmers committing suicide for their inability to pay debts and their incapacitation by the immediate environment.

Social support systems, community counseling centers, value based societies can help protect you. Strong internal reference, beliefs, and empowering values can help from within too.

159

The possible outcomes

❖ Obstacle and failure impact on environment is a certainty, especially in civilized societies like we live in.

❖ The reverse impact of environment on obstacles and failures has more power in comparison to obstacles and failure impact on environment.

❖ The magnitude of impact depends on several factors like culture, region, religion, socio-economic class and several others.

❖ The size and degree of obstacles and failures determines the quantum of impact on the environment.

How to manage

❖ Obstacle and failure impact on environment is not in your control to manage as it depends upon several extraneous factors. Knowing this fact can be advantageous.

❖ Develop skills to encounter, experience, survive and overcome the reverse impact of environment on you, while you struggle with obstacle and failures.

❖ Strong internal reference system with effective beliefs and empowering values focused towards smart goals can help.

❖ Developing abilities to protect from the negative impact of the environment in terms of adversity.

❖ Keeping the company of effective and powerful individuals either as friends or role models can support you to overcome the impact of environment.

"There's no one skill but many which are essential to rise above obstacles and failures, in one's life..."

- Prof.Ram Mohan Rao, Dean, Indian School of Business [ISB]

THE ESSENTIALS

7

THE ESSENTIALS

Arsenal

Just as how a mountaineer will get trained in the trekking institute or a mountaineering school to overcome several obstacles, while attempting to summit the largest peak in the world 'Mount Everest', those of us who have a plan and the will to overcome obstacles in personal, professional and social fronts need thorough preparation to equip for encountering, experiencing, managing and overcoming obstacles and failures.

'The arsenal', I meant symbolically to equip yourself with empowering weapons to summit the internal and external obstacles, you are bound to encounter. The empowering weapons to manage obstacles & failures are right within you and that's why the title.

The below prime weapons are vital for you to feel confident and empowered to overcome the obstacles and failures and are key attributes for success.

Weapon - 1

Empowering Values

It all starts with you possessing 'values' which are founded on deep understanding of your fundamentals and drivers.

If your values are not founded with deeper understanding of your own self, they are bound to be less supported by your beliefs leading to lack of congruence and resulting in 'less power'.

Values which are congruent are formed with deeper understanding of self and are strongly supported by internalized beliefs. They can be referred as 'empowering values' and they present you with clarity and power.

People wonder why Arnold Schwarzenegger despite large obstacles and several failures has not given up or quit on his goals, almost never. So is the case with Mahatma Gandhi, Nelson Mandela and Mother Teresa.

The key is, their values which drive their goals are so deeply founded that nothing external can push them to quit. The power of 'staying the course' despite all odds comes from the 'clarity' and the 'power' to withstand, while supporting one's values.

The weaker majority has neither power nor clarity. Their values are weakly founded and are unsupported in adversity leading to periodic change of goals or even abandoning of the same, several times over.

Weapon-2

Empowering beliefs

No one is born with any beliefs. Most of our childhood is about forming and internalizing beliefs. The 'formative age' is primarily about belief formation and subsequently strengthening of the same by strong references, whether by learning from others or from their own experience of action.

It is necessary that one has empowering beliefs, to manage & overcome obstacles. By focusing on your beliefs and assessing their strength to withstand external influence, can be a step in the right direction, to find if you have 'beliefs' which can support your values.

Beliefs which can support empowering values can be termed 'empowering beliefs'. They need to be founded on strong internal references either by application of your own or of others experiences.

In the times of severe adversities, obstacles and failures, there are instances where only 'beliefs' can act as anchors to stay course and overcome the hard times. Lack of strong internalized empowering beliefs is one of the prime reasons for individuals to quit.

The lack of a strong internalized empowering belief 'I will find options' resulted in Mr. Mir Ranjan Negi to think of suicide as an option, till certain other empowering beliefs came to help him out to redirect his thoughts. If today he's popular, has a movie made on him, and is a television star, and a role model sportsman, and above all 'alive' is because of his 'empowering beliefs'.

Your beliefs could either be 'by default' or 'by design'. I recommend you to periodically pay attention to 'the beliefs' which are supporting your values and driving your goals to check for incongruence and design according to your needs.

There are beliefs which you could choose and internalize consciously to attain empowering beliefs 'by design'.

Weapon-3

SMART Goals

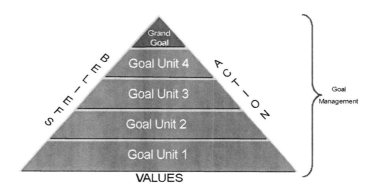

SMART [Simple / Measurable / Achievable / Reviewable / Time Bound] Goals are scientific and logical in the sense; they meet the parameters set by the effective models and are ratified several times by the real accomplishments of individuals from across the spectrum in the world.

SMART Goal example:

"I wish to introduce 2 new members to my Rotary Club, before the end of the June 2008."

The 'Simple' aspect of the goal is, it gives the confidence that it is 'attainable' there by immediate action is possible. Simple also means, there is less or no complexity there by it's easily understood by you and others whose help might need to accomplish the same.

Simple is –

❖ Easy to understand

❖ Easy to measure

❖ Easy to communicate

❖ Easy to share

❖ Easy to delegate

❖ Easy to analyze

❖ Easy to visualize

❖ Easy to strategize

❖ Easy to act on

❖ Easy to feel accomplished

'Measurable' aspect of SMART goal is important to quantify the impact of action, and assess the outcomes. If goals are in absolute terms and are purely qualitative, they can be highly subjective. It cannot be proven to yourself or others that you have accomplished them.

*The 'Two Members' is the measurable aspect in the example above. You can check if you have reached the goal.

'Achievable' – It's important that goals look attainable; more so if they are group goals and involve others support to reach them. Setting goals which look impossible or unrealistic not only demotivates but might also disinterest teams.

*If I were to say 15 members instead of 2, in the above example – It might not appear achievable. Hardly any action is spent on unachievable goals in real.

'Reviewable' – I feel it's very important for the Goals to be flexible enough to make necessary changes, if needed. Reviewable aspect of the goal helps you to change course, change strategy or even change few internal components of the goal to successfully attain it.

'Before the end of June 2008' can give me an opportunity to review in between if I have reached at least a part goal, few months prior to the set date, if not – there is a good possibility, I can extend the date or the number of members in my goal.

"If it was not for focus and perseverance, achieving what I have wouldn't have been possible."

- Rameshwar Rao, Chairman, My Home Group

'Time Bound' – as explained a little in the earlier paragraph. The time bound aspect in the SMART goals, keeps you alert and lets you measure the progress with either the mile stones or through any other form of bench marking. Its important to set time frame on a goal, if not you will never be compelled to act on it.

If I were to say, 'I wish to introduce 2 new members to my Rotary Club'.

It might draw flack from the president of the club, as my goal is aimed infinitely with no time frame, it will neither compel me to act nor interest others involved in the process.

At this juncture, I wish to recommend 'Value Driven SMART Goals' as an effective driver, for you to effectively manage obstacles & succeed.

If your goals are driven from your empowering values and if the GSP is scientific, it's bound to work for you and empower you to manage obstacles & failures effectively.

Model Explanation

As you can see, each goal unit based on the broader frame work of values drives the process. 'Action' and 'Beliefs' support these goals to be accomplished successively and grow further to narrow down to the larger goals and eventually the 'Grand Goal'.

It helps easier goal management, as the progressive growth of accomplishing goals from one goal unit to another, gives ample experience and exposure to you to go towards higher order goals. It's a natural progression towards grand goals, with all the factors of SMART, as explained earlier.

BHAG – [Big Hairy Audacious Goals]

This is an acronym used in lighter vein to identify goals which are set with unscientific and illogical methods; either driven out of exaggerated emotions, or loosely inspired by ineffective role models.

The key characteristic of this goal is its gross success rate. It's so less in comparison to the huge possibility of failure, while pursuing it.

Imagine the number of runaway kids from across the country who land in Mumbai to become the 'Shahrukh Khan' and 'Amithab Bacchan' in Bollywood and you are aware of the success and failure ratio, in these cases. This is a classic example of a BHAG..

In comparison, the SMART goals have very high success rate and the possibility of one accomplishing a SMART goal is almost a 100% if there is effective goal management.

While in BHAG's effective management is almost impossible, as it has no structured basis on which the goals are set.

Key characteristics of BHAG's

❖   Has no Value relevance, at times it could be 100% opposite to the value sequence.

❖   Has no logic, only pure passion [emotion].

❖   Has no support from beliefs, and most of them are external.

❖   Very complex for understanding & explaining to others.

❖   Look and sound unachievable, does not match with skills or knowledge that one has.

❖   Not flexible and usually are one way streets. Do not fit into analysis or strategies.

❖   Never time bound and even if they are defined, possibility is bleak.

❖   Most of them are externally dependent and hardly any internal resources to support.

Just imagine having BHAG's either set unknowingly or living with a set of unconsciously set goals either by you or others, which are neither scientific nor practical. Just imagine the number of obstacles & failures you are inviting and setting yourself up for. God help you :)

Model Explanation

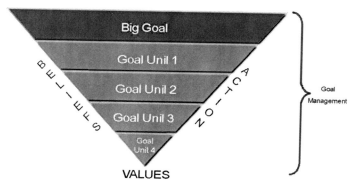

The Inverted pyramid, in any case is unbalanced. As you see this model, you can understand, it is purely driven by one large goal to begin with. It does not graduate from small accomplishments to large.

The beliefs and actions are limiting as the values are least supported in this model. Goal management becomes immensely hard and yet times impossible.

Using 'Value Driven SMART Goals' is one of the key weapons for the summit.

Weapon-4

Emotional intelligence

Obstacles and failures result in 'emotions'. Any possibility of encountering an obstacle can arouse certain emotions, so does the actual experience of facing one. Managing and overcoming obstacles also result in certain key emotions.

Overall, emotions are common factors in the entire process of pre and post obstacle and failure management. Emotions have the capability to create obstacles if mismanaged and also can support you to withstand and overcome obstacles of any size, when well managed. The key for almost all management of obstacles and failures lies in the way one manages his emotions.

Emotions are spontaneous and thereby not very easy to pre manage, I mean prior to feeling them, however the response to emotions can be chosen consciously by a well trained mind, which does not get driven into a reactionary mode at the advent of encountering an obstacle or a failure.

'Gratification' is the basic nature of any individual to react in response to an emotion to satisfy that emotional need.

'Instant Gratification' [IG] is the fastest way to respond to an emotion to satisfy that need. Most of those who would opt for 'IG' are vulnerable to obstacles and failures. They tend to react and thereby minimize options to pro act.

Unleashing fury over a certain obstacle is the result of Instant Gratification. The 'Fragging' incidents in the armed forces which are being reported are a result of reactive expressions to satisfy piled up, unexpressed emotions or letting out all the subdued emotions at once.

171

If you are in the habit of reactively satisfying your emotional needs as they arise, you tend to get into more trouble, in comparison to those, who might take some time and delay gratification of the emotional needs. The primary difference though is to 'Think and Act' than 'Act without thought'. Instant Gratifiers are prone to acting without or less thought.

'Delayed gratification' is a process with which individuals buy ample time to respond to their own and others emotions. Your response is weighed, delayed, well thought of and is consequential. It gives you time to choose more options and to act at an appropriate time for effective results. It is very controlled and thereby very powerful means to overcome obstacle & failure impacts.

Emotional intelligence is a very powerful weapon in the arsenal for individuals who are planning to scale great heights. There are four key stages which represent the Emotional Intelligence.

1.   Self awareness - capability to understand, recognize, and label one's own emotions.

2.   Self regulation - capability to manage and respond to a variety of emotions and needs of one's own self. The restraint to act and the balancing act of feelings and thoughts are the keys.

3.   Social awareness - the capability to recognize, understand and label others emotions and needs. Empathy and active listening are the key attributes.

4.   Social / Relationship management - the capability to manage emotions of one's own self and others by balanced and effective response to the emotional needs of individuals and groups. Trust, empathy, focus, action and balance are the key attributes.

Emotional intelligence as clarified above in brief, is a coveted weapon and a skill you can attain to overcome any adversity.

The hope, desire to succeed, motivation to act, inspiration from role models, pride in winning, confidence, unacceptability of failure, drive, passion are all emotions. As you can see these emotions are key drivers of all obstacle and failure management.

Weapon-5

Healthy physiology

To overcome internal and external obstacles and failures, physical and mental vitality are certainly critical. There is enormous correlation of physiological health to the 'fundamentals and drivers'.

A healthy physiology can present you with more options in comparison to an unhealthy, dilapidated system. The congruence of mind and body in a healthy domain can withstand the rigour of obstacles and failures.

Healthy metabolic activity can trigger a sense of confidence and strength to withstand adversity. The 'fit bodies' and the 'disciplined minds' of sportsmen has strength to withstand massive stress and anxiety. The 'sponge system' absorbs the emotion of failure with an easy reference.

The physiology plays a major role for these men and women to derive strength from within to withstand the hurdles, life presents. I strongly recommend you to read and apply 'Sports Spirit', one of the Summit Models, which will be dealt in chapter 8.

The healthy physiology also means effective and regulated habits, well managed time, empowering values; together this weapon is very critical for managing personal, professional and social obstacles and failures for a long duration of time.

I have known individuals who will wilt like a vegetable encountering the smallest of the obstacles and I also know of men and women who would stand up and live through large obstacles and failures till they overcome them. Physiology surely played a major role in how these individuals handled adversity.

Regular exercise, nutritious habits, active personal work, social life, physically active lifestyle, and engaging occupation will mentally empower you to possess this weapon to manage obstacles and failures.

Weapon-6

Powerful initiative

"Action relates to obstacles. Failure is inadequacy of the effort"
— Prof. Arun Tiwari, Co Author 'Wings of Fire'

There are ways you can respond to adversity, 'you can wait and watch', 'you can withdraw', 'you can quit', or 'you can act'. The options, obstacles and failures present in reference to action are not unlimited, as you can see above there are very few.

The strength is in having 'a powerful initiative', necessarily not meaning that you will jump into action at an advent of an obstacle, but it means 'you will choose to act' eventually when the time is right.

If you possess this weapon, you will not wait, till obstacles or failures compel you.

You will agree that there are individuals who will not act and subsequently turn obstacles into failures. When they realize, they will know the power of 'Initiative.'

Most of the obstacles grow in degree when not acted upon at the early opportunities; if you possess the 'power of initiative', you will have natural willingness to act without being compelled to, by situations.

The measure to assess this factor is to simply look at the number of obstacles you have managed without the 'push to act'. The measure is also possible by looking at the number of failures in one's life and that too of similar types.

Individuals, families, communities and nations at times lack 'power of initiative' and invite larger obstacles resulting in failures. Lack of desire, strength, resolve, goals, clarity and vision can be some reasons for lack of 'initiative'. Most of what it represents is weakness.

There are times a 'mere expression' would have resulted in managing an obstacle while the lack of that small initiative can be blamed for the subsequent growth of the conflict. There are several examples for the above.

On the other hand large obstacles pile up presenting a certainty of failure and yet few nations do not utilize the power of initiative, as a weapon to resolve these long standing obstacles. They set themselves up for failure.

One can never solve or resolve and manage any obstacle, if he doesn't make a conscious beginning. A proactive, planned attempt to override and win an obstacle at the earliest and at an effective stage is critical for deploying this weapon.

Contemplation, postponement, distraction, negligence and lack of focus can minimize power of initiative and result in, you being at the 'receiving end' most of the times.

"If there are no drops, there are no ripples", all result is an outcome of action and the power lies in acting first, when it is the best alternative.

"With my proactive approach, positive outlook and by studying the situation from different angles, I seek to understand & than be understood"

– Seetha Murthy, Principal, Silver Oaks School

Weapon-7

Eagle focus

"For those who are bold and preserving, some channel of success will open up."

- Dr. Y.S.Rajan, Principal Advisor, CII & Co Author of 'Vision 2020' with Dr.A.P.J Kalam

Certain animals and birds especially those which are powerful have this capability to focus on their prey no matter how far or how obscure it might be, they tend to overcome all obstacles to get what they want. Apart from their physical strength, I believe focus as a natural skill, is what gives these animals the edge over others.

In the earlier chapters you have related to how focus and the lack of it can create obstacles. Let's look at how focus can be a potential weapon in the arsenal of an obstacle manager.

If I ask you to look around to find green colored objects around you, you will certainly find few and more persistence can result in a few more. The point is 'focus', when you focus at something and search, eventually you will find what you are searching for.

If your focus is on solution instead on a problem there is a good possibility of you finding the right answers. In contrary, if you are focused on problems you are bound to attract plenty.

Deploying focus as a weapon to overcome obstacles and failures is a smart move as it accentuates and drives more action towards your goal while the lack of it can move it away from goals.

Zeroing in on the 'area of application' in the 'situation environment' to find effective outcomes and while foreseeing potential obstacles and failures is 'eagle focus'.

Knowing what to focus on, where to focus in the clutter of life, is Eagle Focus.

An eagle just does that. Despite how high it flies, eagles focus on its 'area of application (AOA) from a vast 'situation environment', where its prey exists is the key to repeat success of this great bird in its endeavor.

Most of the obstacles at the early stages cry for your focus as most of us are unable to detect or recognize them and can easily overlook to let the obstacle to grow and multiply, resulting in increased gradation of the obstacle to a higher degree. The application of eagle focus on any type and degree of obstacle immediately after one realizes the presence, pays rich dividends.

The ability of effective obstacle and failure managers to avoid distractions, when presented with challenges and their conscious effort to focus on problems at hand mostly turns adversity into an opportunity.

Knowing that you have 'eagle focus' is of great strength for you to brace up and be confident of your capability to address and overcome adversities in your life. It also threatens others who attempt to create hurdles for your progress.

Weapon-8

Balanced Courage

"Courage to think beyond and look for global opportunities is what keeps me and my group going."

– Siva Prasad, Chairman, Matrix Group

Courage is a capability to face and be accountable to the consequences of one's actions. The most courageous people in this world do have fear but they also know how to overcome it. Those who give in and succumb to fear lack courage.

There is a tendency to consider abrasive, adventurous risk taking as courage. The term I intended to use, fit for a weapon is 'balanced courage'.

One's capability to 'rationally' and 'emotionally' analyze consequences of his actions towards goals and unleashing a whole gamut of efforts proactively against all odds is 'balanced courage'.

This factor is crucial for minimizing time bound obstacle impact, as without courage, some actions will lack the speed of decisiveness.

Questions like 'why only few fight against injustice?', 'Why only few aim big?', 'Why are leaders so less in number?', 'Why only few express?' and 'Why is success so scarce?' the answers compel you to think of 'courage'.

Courage is to dream big, work against adversity, plan for eventualities, act with focus and deploy all resources. 'Balanced courage' is about the willingness to act with a predetermined positive outcome in focus and with the strength to face any eventuality in the process.

It is a strong internalized belief system powered by one's confidence, positive experiential reference from the past, compelling goals and clarity of an action plan, clubbed with willingness to initiate action. It's an asset for an obstacle manager especially in the times of higher degree obstacles, failures and adversity.

Columbus, Neil Armstrong, Edmund Hillary, Bachendra Pal, Barack Obama and many other adventurers, wouldn't have taken up initiatives which resulted in historic human victories, if not for 'balanced courage'.

'BC' not just drives large goals but also sustains your pace while you encounter adversities in the process of reaching giant goals.

Weapon-9

Smart Persistence [SP]

"I was persistent & acted consistently for results."

- Mrs. Deepti Reddy, Founder, WOW Hyderabad Magazine

Having all the weapons in the arsenal and not having this will result in not reaching your goals. Most of the obstacles and failures test you to see, if you have this weapon on your side.

As you know persistence is about not giving up. Not quitting. Not deserting or abandoning what you have started. There are instances which are extra ordinary wherein individuals have exhibited exemplary levels of persistence to accomplish their goals.

'Smart persistence' is about knowing how far should you go, how much more you can try, how long you can wait, how much more resources you can deploy, how many more obstacles will you encounter and how many more failures can you stand.

In simple terms the knowledge of your threshold limits in reference to resources, goals and emotions and their implications on the environment around you is 'smart persistence'.

The spirit of persistence remains just the same. The only element which changes is periodic review of 'why persist' and a conscious analysis of new outcomes by trial and error.

The attempt is to bridge the gap between purely emotional connection to a goal and blind faith in results to a balanced approach of both rational and emotional analysis of the resource components in the process.

'Smart persistence' [SP] can also lead to 'stickitivity', which is highly applicable for many young men and women who tend to abandon loyalties to their goals and presuming success in the opposite direction every time they are presented with an obstacle.

There seems to be a pattern of weak behavior, which is prevalent where any small challenge in the form of even trivial obstacle can drive many to quickly switch loyalties and move on. It can be career, relationship, or social goals.

The justification might be saving time and some emotional safety but the loss can be 'conditioning of a new defeating habit' called 'restive abandonment', which means intolerance and restlessness to find options, and abandoning goals of all types in a flash, reactively to move on to some thing else, which might not be of great interest either for a very long time.

The ever increasing divorce rates in India is indicative of the lack of 'SP' and increased 'Restive Abandonment' in the younger population, which has very less persistence to achieve any goals, inclusive of Relationship goals. Increased attrition rates in the IT and ITES sector also reflect a similar handicap.

Weapon-10

Accountable action

There is no alternative to action when it comes to managing obstacles and failures.

Having the entire arsenal means nothing as long as you do not 'act' to overcome the obstacles. Most of the failures in any one's life can be attributed to 'lack of action' towards their goals.

"I deploy burst of activity to overcome crisis, and to gain control of situations."

– V. Agam Rao, Entrepreneur & Educationist

The most demanded, craved for and highly paid attribute of any role is action. No wonder a CEO is the highest paid executive in any organization, as he/she is supposed to drive all action towards organizational goals. Supposed to...

When you take responsibility for all that you 'do', the impact seem to multiply and result in more success. 'Accountable Action' is a term which I have already introduced you to, in the earlier chapters.

"The largest of the wild fires in the world, could have been put off, with single cup of water at the right time."

Even the biggest of obstacle, which is a result of consistent pile up of smaller obstacles mismanaged, can be surmounted with a burst of action units at any time. No wonder, most of our mistakes in the past can be repaired, if we choose to act on them right away, by unleashing massive action for correction. But as the time is the crucial component here, the early the better.

It's natural, when you act; you set into motion, a lot of consequences in several directions, which will drive results. More results mean more options and success is just about that.

"If you are trying to do something, because somebody else is doing...you are inviting trouble."

- Jagapathi Babu, Movie Actor

Failure and obstacles as I have analyzed in the book earlier is mostly the direct implication of 'lack of action'.

In contrary, if you focus on successful individuals, families, communities and nations there is plenty of action, everywhere. Look at India today, action is plenty, its highways are full of trucks transporting goods across the country, there is action in stock markets, action in banks, action in infrastructure, action in entertainment and plenty of action on streets as always.

The same might not be there one day, especially when we pass through a global economic crisis, lack of action in stock markets, lack of action in banks are the prime results of the slow down, lack of action is usually a sign of an obstacle or failure in any sense.

The new age India is all about action and no wonder, the foreigners who visit India are captivated by so much that happens here.

Imagine a nation, where there is poverty all over, failure all over, violence all over, and is in turmoil, there will be very less action and specially 'Accountable Action'. I hope, I have driven home the point.

Accountable Action is growth

The power of this weapon is double edged, if you unleash unaccountable action units without investment of thought, plan and resource support, they will result in highly ineffective outcomes.

While consistent Accountable Action can be a very powerful weapon to overcome any obstacle and failure and lead you to immense growth possibilities.

I urge you to measure your power in this area by assessing the amount of Accountable Action applied in the recent past and the subsequent results. All success over obstacles and failures in your life is directly connected to the amount of Accountable Action you undertake.

"Different methods yield different results. All pervasive obstacles & failures in life need to be handled with precision and creative methods, to overcome and to succeed".

- Prof. Gale Naughton, Dean, School of Business,
Sandiego State University, SDSU

THE SUMMIT

THE SUMMIT

After reading the last seven chapters you would have by now gained lot of insight for systematically demystifying various layers of obstacles and understood their impact on several dimensions of your personal and professional life.

The earlier chapters holds the key for all that you are planning to apply, to SUMMIT your Everest's both internally and externally. This chapter is like the heart of watermelon, more raved for and convenient to eat, but one has to cut through the thicker surface and several layers of fruit to get here.

'The first step for a man and a giant leap for the mankind' was the outcome of accomplishing a grand goal of a man setting foot on the moon for the first time.

I present to you 8 giant steps, which I am sure would have been applied by all those who have achieved grand goals in their lives, changing everyone's lives around them. These are easy steps to practice and turn into habits, once they are your habits, there's no stopping you. Keep Walking.

Giant Step-1

The Big Picture Vision

"I always think big and believe it's possible to achieve. And most often than not, I am right."

— Mrs. Seeta Murthy, Principal, Silver Oaks School

While I profiled several categories of obstacle attractors, you would have figured out a vital commonality in all of them 'lack of big picture vision'.

Narrow understanding of important aspects of one's life and at times ignorance of how wide the horizon is, can lead to habitual conditioning of 'minimal thinking'.

Starting from 'top-down approach' is advisable in reference to your perspective, than 'bottom-top approach', the later can lead to dismal comprehension capability of how large the canvas of life is, and how small the obstacles we face, in comparison are. The former approach takes a look at your life from the space and understands its grandeur, purpose and what a great opportunity to live is.

Most obstacles are the outcomes of your perception and depending on the basis of your fundamentals and drivers; you will perceive your obstacles. No wonder individuals whose obstacles either overwhelm them or drive them into deprivation have issues with their fundamentals and drivers.

In this step to summit, you will either naturally or by design, think from the macro viewpoint to view the obstacles with a large perspective and not a narrow one. You will not forget the bigger picture; you will understand that the large goal lies beyond these obstacles. You will realize, in comparison to joy of reaching the larger goal one day, any obstacle is too small to stop you in between.

For example, a sales executive whose grand goal is to head the department finally and has clarity of that goal with a well designed action plan, his perception of impediments and obstacles on the field will be quite different in comparison to one with a smaller goal. The one who has the grand goal will have the big picture vision.

"I truly believe that if I get to the root of any obstacle, I can overcome it. 'Wiping a wound' does not heal it. I have to know the 'why' and 'how' of it, to resolve it."

– Rahul Bajaj, MBA, Young Management Professional

The idea is to build the spirit to manage obstacles by making them look smaller in comparison to the larger goal, even before reaching it.

Coleman York, a dear friend and the Country Manager of the sales organization, I got trained at the beginning of my career, used to always motivate the teams by a very visual success outcome, his Porsche 911 car, he used to say "You have to go through many shut doors and negatives to get to drive a Porsche".

Those of us, who related to his 'big picture vision', have considerably improved our sales through capable handling of obstacles by making them look smaller, in comparison to the Porsche, which we would get to drive one day. Infact, when I visited USA in 1997 for a sales rally, I made sure I drove a Porsche of a friend, to realize that small dream I had, then.

Lack of big picture vision can lead you to experience intimidation even at the smallest obstacle management and there is immense possibility of quitting your goals.

Those who complain, crib, wimp and blame while encountering an obstacle need to pay attention to the overall process of obstacle management more closely to attain this competence.

Apply this Giant Step

❖ Have a grand goal

❖ Have clarity of smaller goal sets.

❖ Relate and visualize success outcomes of the grand goal.

❖ Relate and visualize outcomes of smaller goal sets.

❖ Increase the power of visualization.

❖ Virtually live or experience the success outcomes of the grand goal even before reaching it.

❖ Relate and follow role models who are living your dreams already.

Giant Step-2

Sports Spirit

"I have never understood failure; I always felt there will be a second chance to win."

– Mukesh Kumar, Former Captain, Indian Hockey

Developing 'Sports Spirit' can be a step in the right direction at this stage. You will agree professional sportsmen are a different breed, when it comes to obstacle and failure management.

In my personal interactions with nationally and internationally popular sports men and women for the book, I started realizing how different their perception of success, obstacle and failure is in comparison to others. Their everyday encounter with obstacles, failures and even success, makes them realize the temporariness of each of these events.

Yes! You are right, that's how they perceive SOF [Success, Obstacles & Failure] as 'An Event'.

"Failure is only when you give up and quit. As long as you are in the game, you can always be successful the next time around."

- Prem Chand Degra, Mr. Universe, Professional Body Builder

Key Characteristics -

❖   Their healthy, well exercised bodies / Healthy Physiology

❖   Their focus on SMART goals and Grand Goals.

❖   Their Self Motivation to reach goals and Coache's support system.

❖   The support system from team mates and fans.

❖   Their constant exposure to effective role models and coaches, who are winners.

❖   Active life style, where one does not get time to brood over yesterday's failure.

❖ The competitiveness, to stay in the game to win another day.

❖ Their belief that 'You will win some and lose some'.

❖ Their tryst with win/lose opportunities through competitions and championships very often, gets them enough experiences and prepares them to cope.

The above system endows a sportsman with a very special skill set, which mostly is natural to all great sportsmen 'strength to withstand defeat'.

Sports Spirit is – 'The ability to perceive success, obstacles and failures as very normal events in everyday life and initiate quick acceptance and quick search for solutions to manage the same. It is also about staying focused to win at all odds with strong internalized beliefs. And plenty of discipline.'

Learn to take this step, for Summiting your Everest, and you will find, nothing on your way, can hinder your progress. The sports spirit can keep you alive in the most testing adversities that you might face in your life. 'Winning and losing is all in the game.'

"Obstacles are much easier to handle in my business today, as I am a sportsman and have lived through obstacles every day. They don't bother me much. I just focus on my goals."

> \- Nadeemuddin, Corporate Fitness Coach,
> CEO, Active Life Consulting

Apply this Giant Step

❖ Play a sport of your choice; better still become a part time professional sports man.

❖ Follow Sportsmen and their success stories.

- ❖ Find Role models in the area of sports.

- ❖ Focus on quick acceptance and resolution.

- ❖ Focus on healthy physiology.

- ❖ Get into highly active lifestyle.

- ❖ Exercise regularly.

- ❖ Build discipline into your everyday life.

- ❖ Practice all that stands for 'Sports Spirit'.

Giant Step-3

Exercising Options

Have you ever solved a problem without thinking of 'all the possible solutions'? Searching for possibilities to solve a problem, issue or a situation will result in options; I call them 'choices' for ease of use.

"Listening to the coach, getting professional guidance, trusting the instruction and going behind goals with passion are the keys to managing obstacles for sportsmen."

- Adhikari, Mr.India, Professional Body Builder & Coach

This method of managing obstacles is one of the highest in the order of actions, but a very basic step forward. Without taking this step, you cannot move forward to 'Summit'.

I have seen several individuals who are so occupied and deeply involved, that they are visually in the heart of an obstacle not outside it. If you are engulfed by an obstacle, your capability to find 'choices' to solve are minimal.

You will find many choices, even in the most complex adversity, when you are willing to exercise your 'power to choose'.

The 'power of exercising choices', comes from a disassociated, non reactive, composed and objective mindset. It is sometimes sad to find individuals choked or frozen by an obstacle so much, that they fail to recognize the availability of choices all around them.

"I was trained early in martial arts to overcome my innermost fears about my opponent, once I am fearless inside, I can take on anyone in the ring. I try to apply this every day in my real life situations."

– Kashif Suleman, Celebrity Martial Arts Trainer & Actor

There are several cases that I have seen and may be several, which you would have experienced where 'the capability to choose' is drastically reduced by the reactive tendencies of an individual encountering an obstacle.

You can possibly pick the worst possible options at that time and act on it, instead of best. You would not do it, if you were to know the availability of that option; you might have found only one, and acted upon it. Early marriage divorces are a classic example.

The summiteers of the large obstacles are proactively and consistently trying to find more choices, various methods and ways to overcome an obstacle at hand. Their incessant, refined, focused and surgical search for choices gives them plenty of options for success.

Apply this Giant Step

❖ Realize that you are an adult and you have the power to choose.

❖ Be controlled in your response to the first encounter of an obstacle, do not react.

❖ Look at an obstacle from a distance and detach yourself from its effect.

❖ Ask a question 'what are my choices under the given circumstances.' And ask it as many times as you can.

❖ Ask a question 'what will I do if I were...', Fill in your role model's name.

❖ Decisively make choices, which are effective.

❖ Fearlessly choose what is best for you and act on it.

Giant Step-4

Perceptive Attitude

There are individuals who will act as if 'they have already attained the success of their grand goals', while there are few who despite attaining success at smaller goal sets, simply move on to the next goal mechanically without celebrating the success of reaching a goal.

"I think life is what you make of. I always try to think big and play with many choices to make it bigger and better always."

- Hamed Saberi, Chairman & Managing Director, Shades

There is nothing wrong with the latter except that he might face a huge obstacle and might not have enough steam left to fight it, as there is a possibility of getting tired of scaling the peak forever.

'Acting a winner' has never hurt anyone; you are only living a future role, which you will make it a possibility by working hard towards it. You can exude the confidence of the winner even prior to being one, you are actually exhibiting your deepest desire to win, which can help you overcome certain obstacles, which require a higher sense of achievement and confidence, which you already possess, while living that role.

'Perceptive Attitude' is not a mere deception or a facade, but a very smart step forward, to experience success prior to actually accomplishing the same. I remember many children sitting in the father's rocking chair and acting as their father, to show their quest to grow up fast. It's natural.

I chose to fly from Bangalore to Hyderabad, while I was just 6 months into my first job and way before I actually could afford it. I wanted that experience, to push me to accomplish larger goals, so that I can actually fly frequently without strain on my budgets. This eventually turned true right after one year of persistent action towards my goal. I am talking about almost 12 years back.

There are several men and women who have overcome largest obstacles by putting to use this method to gain confidence and strength in the times of adversity.

Al Pacino, not a very tall man but a super star of Hollywood actually 'feels tall', while he acts his scenes, which reflects in his confidence and poise on screen when pitted against taller actresses and other taller co-stars.

His method of overcoming a physical obstacle 'short height' through a perceptive attitude of 'I am tall enough' works for him, to overcome that obstacle. His consistent success at box office though is connected to his acting capabilities and the confidence is obtained from a powerful method of 'perceptive attitude' which makes him look sometimes taller than the tallest of his fellow actors.

"Sportsman has this spirit of washing off failure at their locker room showers and be fresh for the next game. Ofcourse the one who learns from the failure before rinsing off is the one, who wins next."
- Prof. Adrian Kennedy, Managing Director, Wellness RX Apollo

There is an old method to not get attacked by any dog. This is how it works. When you are walking past it, act as if 'that dog means nothing to you', 'it does not exist' and 'you care two hoods for it.' Surprisingly 99 out of 100 times, you may succeed passing through, without even getting barked at, try it at your risk, it works. If you act the 'perceptive attitude' with ease and full faith, it works for me, all the time.

I know by now you figured out what this method is all about. It's about believing strongly that you will overcome a certain obstacle and exhibiting that belief externally through your feelings, thoughts and actions.

Apply this Giant Step

❖   Develop a strong belief of overcoming an obstacle.

❖   Express that belief through your feelings, thoughts and actions.

❖   Measure the impact of your attitude in overcoming the obstacle in real time.

❖ Record 'what works and what doesn't work' in reference to the perceptive attitude.

❖ Reinforce your beliefs of managing an obstacle every time you overcome one.

❖ Draw strength from perceptive success outcomes prior to overcoming an obstacle.

❖ Live your dream [at least in your mind], before you actually achieve it in real.

Giant Step-5

Challenging the Comfort Zone

"My setbacks definitely are of highest order when I was dubbed as traitor after our national hockey team lost to Pakistan in 1982 Asian games final. I was branded as traitor and friend of Pakistan. It was extremely difficult. Then sometimes back I lost my young son in a road accident. It was really heart breaking. But then I am not the one who accept defeat so easily. I am a fighter and have always resurrected myself from ashes."

- Mir Ranjan Negi, Former Captain, Indian Hockey

It is a very important step to summit. Most often than not, smaller obstacles unattended, pile up to become larger obstacles which can compel failures. Initiative to act while the obstacles are still smaller can help to avert this danger.

Many individuals find very less motivation from within to attack and overcome an obstacle at its infancy. The reason can be one's comfort levels in not acting or finding pleasure in the status quo or possessing smaller goals.

There are several comfort zones in us internally, which many of us fail to identify and I'll list out few of the comfort zones and the prospective obstacles, if these comfort zones are not challenged, for your reference.

❖ 'I am too lazy, to be very active' is a comfort zone, if not challenged, can lead to several health, relationship, professional, activity and competence related obstacles.

❖ 'I already know too much' is a comfort zone, if not challenged can lead to lack of professionalism, stunted growth, closed mind, narrow knowledge, strained relationships, social misgivings as some of the obstacles.

❖ 'I like to work at my own pace', this ineffectively formed comfort zone can lead to lack of large goals, lack of respect, mismanagement of resources, wastage of time, lack of growth as some obstacles.

❖ 'I have money, so all's well' is a comfort zone, which can impact your relationships, without your knowledge as you will neglect the 'respect' and 'trust' building actions, as your focus is comfortably in money. Relationship and Social obstacles can be a great possibility.

❖ 'I have accomplished everything' is a comfort zone, which can kill enterprise, smarts, activity and new goals in one's life, can lead to personal, financial, health and social obstacles.

❖ 'Why should I initiate the dialogue' is a comfort zone, which many couples face on a daily basis and this can lead to small issues piling up to grow into large relationship obstacles. This comfort zone expects one individual in a relationship to always initiate a 'patch up' resulting in loss of interest to repair from one end, all the time.

❖ 'I am like this only' is a very dangerous comfort zone of close minded individuals, who are bound to face immense obstacles in their life, with their brittle personalities, which do not transform to accommodate change. Most of the personal conflicts in spousal relationships, work relationships are rooted at this attitude of 'why should I change?' without applying any logic to understand, if there is a 'need to change'.

Likewise, there are several comfort zones you might have, and the best way is to find them from your daily and weekly reviews.

"Most of my childhood troubles are attributed to me being not in a position to make choices and others were making it or forcing it on me, while I was growing up. Freedom to make choices now, almost feels like a new life"

-Mrs.Pratibha Sagar,Home Maker, Director, Matrix Mentoring

There are many comfort zones like inhibitions, less urge to express, deceptive outlook, focus only on wealth, egotism, close mind, lack of initiative, sedentary lifestyles, workaholism, idling and many several more, which can attract obstacles and also reduce the capability of individuals to manage the same.

Challenging comfort zones is one of the key summit attributes; those who summit their 'Everest' within and outside, have challenged and broke their comfort zones several times over. No question about it. When are you breaking yours?

One needs to recognize his own comfort zones in reference to his personal, professional, social and global goals and challenge them to break free of the same.

Organizational Application

"Even in the competitive arena of business, I have let the flow take me over and lead me to the simple satisfaction of doing a job well. I could never have found happiness by stepping on someone else's toes. To me 'flow' implies immersing oneself fully into what one does. It is characterized by a feeling of energized focus, genuine involvement, and success in the process of the activity. The flow gets empowered as one manages to create a balance between the tangible and the intangible, which is so essential to survive in the world we live today."

– Kishore Biyani, Chairman, Future Group

'I feel safe , if I am silent' is one of the comfort zones of a professional attending a review meeting, can lead to many obstacles in the form of miscommunication between the team members, lack of contribution, lack of bonding, accountability and professionalism which can potentially result in team failures.

Organizations need to focus on the impact of organizational comfort zones, leading to obstacles in the areas of their strategic growth factors such as lack of business expansion, lack of creativity and the lack of drive to reach large goals.

Apply this Giant Step

❖ Assess and review all your weaknesses to see, if there are any comfort zones driving them.

❖ Analyze the depth of your comfort zones by checking applications of action, against these zones periodically.

❖ Assess the impact of your comfort zones on your action units and measure the resource misutilization in the process of achieving smaller goal units.

❖ Pay attention to all the obstacles you encounter and establish direct linkages to your comfort zones.

❖ Identify if some of your routines could potentially be comfort zones, depriving you of creativity and new direction and new goals.

❖ Register and record several past 'managed obstacles' and check if challenging and breaking certain comfort zones was one of the key action units to have overcome.

Giant Step-6

Comparative Strokes

"There's nothing which equals positive attitude, when you aim to achieve something very big."

— Dr. A.P.J.Abdul Kalam, Former President of India

It is important to pay attention to this summit method, as it is laced with a hint of philosophy and plenty of scientific approach.

It is necessary that we understand a 'stroke' prior to attempting to practice this method for 'Summiting your Everest'. A stroke is a set of words aligned to compliment a purpose which is predetermined and with a predetermined result expected in return. It is primarily an expression aimed with an expectation of clear predetermined results.

"I am of the view, if you make up your mind to do 'what ever it takes' to reach your goal, you will one day get there. There should not be any reservations & limitations. I follow it."

- Rahul Dev, Actor

There are several types of strokes depending upon the need for effectiveness for achieving certain objectives. It can be a simple stroke, a conditional stroke, an unconditional stroke and could also be conditional positive and conditional negative.

'I like you' is a simple stroke, it is also an unconditional stroke.

'I like you more, when you smile' is a conditional stroke.

In this case, the former is a simple expression of liking, precisely directed for attaining its purpose-'fulfill the need to express liking'. To make someone feel good or secure or complimented can be the purpose.

In the latter case it is an expression of liking directed for attaining its purpose to change behaviors, the change in behavior expected is a 'smile'.

'I don't like you, when you don't smile' is a negative conditional stroke, which attempts to attain its purpose through instilling fear.

"It temporarily scars personal relationships. But then there is day after every night. It is the cardinal truth."

- Mir Ranjan Negi, Former Captain, Indian Hockey

Most of the expression related issues can lead you to relationship obstacles in personal, professional, family, social and global environments.

In this method to summit, comparative strokes is a process of comparing one's obstacles to that of others, who have more obstacles than you and finding solace to one's own situation of having comparatively less.

'I am better off than a million others' is an effective comparative stroke which can help you, in the times of adversity to minimize the impact.

"I was facing a large obstacle in my professional life, years ago and one day, I have met this mother with a small baby suffering from cancer. My obstacle looked tiny & trivial."

- Jagapathi Babu, Movie Actor

In contrary, ineffectiveness of individuals managing obstacles lies in their comparison to others 'who have fewer obstacles than them'. They can feel burdened by that comparison.

'I am in a worse position, than so many I know' can lead to dismal handling of obstacles as they tend to incapacitate and take strength away from an individual facing adversity.

Comparative stroke is a very powerful tool for summiting the Everest as attitude of 'I can do it, if he can do it', is an effective comparison for managing obstacles related to motivation, confidence and competence.

Apply this Giant Step

❖　It is important to develop an effective orientation to choose right words to define an obstacle. The choice of wrong words can inflate and exaggerate the dimensions of an obstacle.

❖　The ability and maturity to compare to people in better position than you for drive and motivation, and compare to people in lower positions than you for satisfaction, strength and confidence is vital for obstacle management.

❖　'I am just a drop in an ocean', 'I am a tiny particle in the entire universe', 'I am better off than those in Iraq today', 'I at least have a job and many doesn't even have one', are some of the comparative strokes which can give strength in the times of adversities.

High Utility Positive Strokes -
In the times of Adversity

❖　Strokes such as 'Everything happens for a reason ', 'there is no gain without pain' , 'there is always another day', 'there is a rainbow amidst dark clouds', are some of the positively compelling strokes which can protect and strengthen one's resolve to overcome obstacles.

❖　'This too, shall pass' is a very powerful stroke to highlight the temporariness of an obstacle or a failure phase.

Giant Step-7

Visualization

"Visualization is a very effective tool, to overcome obstacles and failures. I have applied it several times to overcome obstacles."
– Dr. A.P.J. Abdul Kalam, Former President of India

This step to summit obstacle and failures is a very critical competence which some of us naturally possess and some need to focus heavily.

The ability to foresee a predetermined outcome or a result with precision and specific visual details on your mind's screen is 'visualization'.

To attain success at a smallest goal unit to the largest of grand goal, this competence can influence very effectively. There are hardly any leaders who have attained greatness through managing insurmountable obstacles, who haven't applied visualization as one of the methods to overcome the times of adversity.

Is there anything more compelling than a detailed vision of living your dream even prior to actually accomplishing the same? Think about it.

I know several men and women from different walks of life who have visualized their success, even in the midst of overwhelming adversity and who have eventually overcome those obstacles and attained success.

Mahatma Gandhi's visual capability was so enormous and so evident that every time he spoke, it reflected the future imagery in detail of a free India. If you follow his speeches, you will be able to associate his visual sense of how he could see 'Free India' decades prior to actually attaining it in real.

I personally feel, its ironic that Mahatma Gandhi did not live 'The real free India' after independence for that long, while he lived there for decades in his dreams. Visualization, I strongly believe, is what kept him going despite all the obstacles which are humanly impossible to overcome, for decades.

Whether it's Bill Gates, Dhirubhai Ambani or Lakshmi Mittal who have attained global success in business, I am sure they would have applied lot of visualization to reach their grand goals. It's almost impossible to live through adversity; survive and reach grand goals without having the capability to visualize success on the other side of these daunting hurdles.

While the above examples are of 'effective visualization', there is a lurking danger in individuals having an 'ineffective visualization' driven through ineffective feelings, values and beliefs.

You can assess the amount of damage 'ineffective visualization' can cause. Imagine someone's capability to see an obstacle and a failure to a minute detail and have the visual capability to blow it out of proportion. Most of the overwhelming obstacles which unsettle, scare and depress us are the outcomes of ineffectively projected visuals of obstacles and failures on our mind screen.

I urge you to pay attention to what your visualization is focused at 'reaching grand goals' or 'the specifics of obstacles'. And you know what is better to visualize, for overcoming adversity.

Apply this Giant Step

❖   Check if you have the ability to visualize your goals.

❖   Check if you have the ability to visualize attaining your goals.

❖   Increase your visualization capability by regular practice.

❖   Do not under estimate the 'power of effective visualization'.

❖   Share the details of your vision to select few for focused commitment to attain goals.

❖   Feel validated and celebrate attaining visualized success every time you do.

❖   Calibrate for precision of visuals and make it a habit.

❖   Self discipline, active physiology, meditation and pleasant environment can enhance 'effective visualization'.

Giant Step-8

Intention [Vs] Behavior

> *"I see myself at the finished line before anyone else"*
> – Carl Lewis, Former World Champion, 100 Meters Sprint

As we are aware by now, that all obstacles and failures are the creatures of our own perception, there is a huge possibility of individuals resurrecting large obstacles out of nothing.

This method of summit helps you analyze 'your judgement and assessment of self and others', to constructively avert obstacles and failures through judgement mishaps.

Most of the relationship obstacles in all the personal, professional and social categories are primarily driven out of our judgement of situation and behavior of others in a transaction. And mostly the process of this judgement is driven out of a habitual conditioned mechanism.

Many of us are conditioned to judge others by their 'behavior' alone and ourselves with 'intention' alone. It's very convenient method and very popular in its usage, think about it...

"I think most of us do fall prey to noble intentions and lack of control over one's behavior. I feel both are equally important"
— Manish Kumar Malpani, Executive Director, Maheshwari Group

When someone yells at me, 'he is rude' is our judgement of the other person and thereby 'rude' is the label we assign to that individual. This judgement, if based on wrong analysis can eventually result in a relationship obstacle or sometimes even a relationship failure. Am I right?

Let's play the same scenario, a little differently now.

While you yell at others, do you judge your behavior as 'Rude' too, I hope not.

You will justify your behavior with your 'intentions'. You will exclaim 'My intention is to correct you'.

So, when someone else's actions are rude and the same actions turn noble when you express, exhibits the bias in judging yourself to others which can potentially lead to many obstacles and failures in relationships.

The ideal though, is to judge both 'self' and 'others' with one measure. Both by 'intention and behavior' and in that specific order, no matter how noble your intentions are, you need to keep a check on your behavior with others, the same measure holds good for others too.

To summit large obstacles, one needs to possess the semblance and maturity to objectively assess one's own misgivings and others, to make effective judgements for needed action.

Apply this Giant Step

❖　　Avoid reactive and fast paced judgements on self and others.

❖　　Give time for you to objectively assess and judge people and situations, don't jump into conclusions.

❖　　Learn to forget and forgive to reduce 'mental luggage', especially which is trivial.

❖　　Focus on both intention and behavior to judge people in any transaction.

❖　　Focus on intention and behavior to judge you in any situation or transaction.

❖　　Have courage to admit mistakes and be open to corrections by others.

❖　　Be driven to have constructive and positive intentions, which are aligned with your goals.

Giant Step-9

Model Explanation

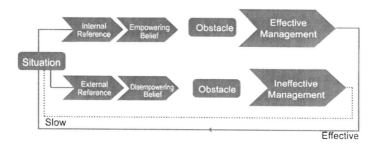

The above model shows that If 'empowering beliefs' are internalized and are used as effective references the obstacle management is effective and while the 'disempowering beliefs' are applied, there is a slow down in the process of obstacle management and can possibly lead to mismanagement of obstacles and the situation.

Reference Management

"Deeper the setback more is my will to come back. Not to prove something to someone but to keep myself on right track. Pathway to success is always full of thorns. I believe winners always tread a path that is less traversed by others".

– Mir Ranjan Negi, Former Captain, Indian Hockey

Most of what you believe you can do, or you cannot arise from our references to certain role models. It is indisputable that most of our capabilities to either manage or mismanage obstacles come from our references from past, present or future.

209

'I don't think I can overcome that obstacle' is driven out of a past reference or simply a past experience of your own or others experience you are relating to.

'Nobody has ever stepped on moon, so I can't do it' was the reference prior to Neil Armstrong stepping on the moon.

'Neil did it, I can do it too' was the immediate reference of many astronomers, who ventured to land on moon after him. What was impossible earlier quickly turned possible with one 'effective reference'.

The same could be true for 'ineffective references'. You can relate to one of your past experience of failure and consider every time you attempt similar action you would fail. It sucks 'courage' out of your system and disempowers you. This could also happen with your strong reference to others failure.

"If Rupert Murdoch can be the Media Mogul, I can be too one day for sure."

— Ravi Prakash, CEO, TV9

The wife of a good friend in Ohio, Columbus has experienced two accidents while she was driving her car, in a span of two months in a winter season. I could personally see her strong references to 'what she considered her failure' in her driving competence, resulted in losing complete confidence to drive again.

It's almost three years now and she's still scared of getting behind the wheel. Imagine the impact of an 'ineffective reference' and its 'power' to set up obstacles in your path and undermine your ability to overcome.

I hope by now you are aware of the intensity and power of 'reference management' has on your obstacle and failure management capability. Having effective role models can immensely help in building a strong effective reference system and build resistance to adversity and obstacles.

Apply this Giant Step

❖ Focus on 'your role models' in past, present and future and assess their orientation, strength and impact.

❖ Pay attention to your memory of your past experiences and check for 'ineffective references'.

❖ Always try connecting with 'effective references', especially at the time of adversity.

❖ Check for social conditioning impacting your 'references'.

❖ Act on establishing effective role models in all dimensions of your life for strong reference management.

❖ Read, follow and relate to effective references regularly for strengthening your reference framework for reaching grand goals.

TIME TO ACT

I am glad that you have read the entire book. You must be now very well aware of your own internal definitions of Success, Obstacles and Failure and realized the need for redefining those definitions for attaining your grand goals.

For a life as grand as we humans have, it works to set grand goals to serve the purpose and add value to the world we live in. Grand Goals as you have figured out by now, not just helps you attain great heights but keep you going, when the toughest obstacles descend on you.

The time to act is now -

❖ Give yourself a break and spend few hours or a day just with yourself.

❖ Apply the newly acquired knowledge on 'Fundamentals' & 'Drivers' to your own personality & life.

❖ Look at the strengths, gaps, shortcomings, conditioning and fallacies, act with understanding of the above.

❖ Take control of your life right away by acting on piled up / postponed obstacles which needed your attention.

❖ Review your goals and assess their GSP [Goal Setting Process] as explained in the book and see if your goals are set with congruence.

❖ Review all your obstacles and apply the 'Weapons' and 'Giant Steps' and see them disappear, as you get equipped to manage them successfully.

❖ Act towards your goal units with clarity of thought and suitably redefined definitions of Success / Obstacle & Failure.

❖ Act now to increase the macro view point on your life, and all those small events disguised as obstacles & failures, which challenge you on the journey to reach your grand goals.

❖ Act now to gain support of your family, well wishers, friends and community to build a solid support system to lean on in the times of adversity. Care for them and they will surely return it, when you need the most.

And ofcourse keep this coach 'Summit Your Everest' handy for regular reference for successfully overcoming your obstacles and failures. In case you, your family, your colleagues or your organization needs any support in the form me, I am just a call or an email away.

Thank you for scaling this 'Summit' along with me. I will look forward to seeing you soon.

Your coach,

Krishna Sagar

AUDIO TRAINING CD'S

Grab your copy or gift some one you love the world class training sessions in Krishna Sagar's voice.

Order Now

❖ Empower Your Decision Making

❖ Emotional Intelligence-Part# 1

❖ Effective Communication

❖ Successful Relationship Management

Each Title @ Rs.100/-

Contact: media@matrixnova.com

STAY IN TOUCH & SPEAK OUT

❖ Write your observations, feedback, testimonials or even criticism personally to the author Krishna Sagar at : sagar@matrixnova.com

❖ Join the 'weekly mailer' & receive free inspirational messages and solutions from Krishna Sagar every week. E-mail at: wm@matrixnova.com

❖ Join Krishna Sagar at Face book- Just type in the handle in the search box- 'Krishna Sagar Rao'

❖ Buy the book online or ship it to your friends anywhere in the world, follow the Book's progress / Reader's Testimonials / Download Freebies by visiting : www.summityoureverest.com

❖ Keep track of Krishna Sagar's Seminars / Events & Speaking Sessions by visiting: www.ksagar.com / www.matrixnova.com

LaVergne, TN USA
28 October 2009
162340LV00005B/152/P